MANSIONS OF THE SOUL
THE COSMIC CONCEPTION

Mansions of the Soul

The Cosmic Conception

by
H. Spencer Lewis

AMORC

Published by the Grand Lodge of the
English Language Jurisdiction, AMORC, Inc.
1342 Naglee Avenue • San Jose, CA 95191
www.rosicrucian.org

First Hardbound Edition, 1930
© 1930 and 1954 by Supreme Grand Lodge of AMORC, Inc.
All Rights Reserved

©1996, Supreme Grand Lodge of the Ancient & Mystical Order
Rosae Crucis
Published by the Grand Lodge of the English
Language Jurisdication, AMORC, Inc.

Library of Congress Catalog Card No.: 30-034218

First Paperbound Edition, 1986

ISBN 0-912057-43-2

10 9 8 7 6

Printed and bound in U.S.A.

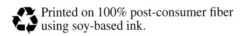 Printed on 100% post-consumer fiber
using soy-based ink.

DEDICATION

To the Fearlessness and Frankness of
H. F.
who has so often and convincingly expressed his
faith in the Doctrines of Reincarnation, and
who has demonstrated his complete trust
in these principles by his broad
vision, human sympathy, and
unlimited plans for
the future.

This Book is Dedicated
with the wish that his marvelous industrial
achievements may continue to have
the well-deserved Cosmic
Benediction and
Blessing.

CONTENTS

INTRODUCTION

The continued interest in the Western world regarding the religions and religious wisdom and philosophies of other lands has led many thinking persons to give serious consideration to the very old and logical doctrine of reincarnation.

The demand for some understandable and rational explanation of the doctrine of reincarnation is responsible for the publication of this book. There are many small books or pamphlets in the libraries of the Western world today dealing with the subject of reincarnation, but in nearly every instance these books have been written and issued in conjunction with the outline of some ancient mystical religion. For this reason most of them are filled with strange philosophical terms or mystical principles which make the fundamentals of reincarnation difficult to understand and difficult to accept.

Perhaps this is why so many of those who are devout students of the modern Christian or the modern Jewish religions hesitate to accept any of the principles of reincarnation. I have yet to find an intelligent man or woman who, after hearing the true doctrines of reincarnation properly presented, refuses to admit that they are reasonable, logical, and acceptable.

With this in mind, therefore, the chapters of this book were prepared at various times as inspiration moved me to write.

This much can be said in closing any argument regarding the truthfulness or soundness of the doctrine of reincarnation. We are here on this earth plane living a life of trials, experiences, lessons, and constructive instruction. Whether we accept the doctrine of reincarnation or not we will continue to live in accordance with some law, some principle, some scheme of things; and, when the end comes, this period of life on earth will be consummated and through transition we will learn of what there is in the future. What we may believe, or think, in regard to reincarnation will not change one principle of the doctrine nor affect the laws involved one iota. The great effect of such belief or disbelief, or the acceptance or non-acceptance of these doctrines, will be in our lives as we are living them *here* and in our readiness and preparation to meet transition when we come face to face with it.

Knowing, therefore, that the acceptance of these doctrines will bring to the reader, as it has brought to millions of others, greater happiness in life through a greater understanding of the trials and problems involved, and an absolute fearlessness of so-called death, I close my manuscripts and pass them on to the mechanical masters who will prepare them for the public, and rest in the hope that thousands may find *Light, Life, and Love* through what I have written.

—H. Spencer Lewis.

The Temple of Alden,
San Jose, California.
September 15, 1930.

CHAPTER 1

"I GO TO PREPARE A PLACE FOR YOU"

The stone was struck and there issued a spark! Again the striking of the stone, and another spark! And a third time! Now a little flame grew in the dry grass and feathers; and the flame gave forth light and burned the little twigs, producing a fire. The fire was kindled and nourished until it enlarged its size and intensity. Burning on flat stones and crudely protected by others, there was soon a small furnace of heat and light which radiated its vibrations into the gloom of the small wood-and-mud cabin.

Rejoicing in this new and marvelous addition to their roughly constructed home, primitive man and primitive woman, for the first time, seated themselves on the bark-covered floor and gazed into the dimly lighted recesses of the enclosure which now became an enjoyable place at night.

Not long ago, this man and woman had ventured from the protected place in the branches of a tree, where they had lived in safety, to construct and occupy the dream place of their evolving minds. Contemplating the possibility of a larger environment than the tree afforded for safe relaxation and protection from animals of prey, they had built the first home, the first cottage, the first castle man ever knew.

With the setting of the sun each day came darkness and the coldness of the night. The long hours of silence, accompanied by the inability to see or to employ the time, added to the despondency and discouragement of the monotonous life from sunset to sunrise. True, the more perfect enclosure and protection from winds and storms made this crude home so superior to the dwelling place in the trees that a sense of kingship and mastership over the elements and the creatures of the earth brought many new inspirations to the minds and hearts of these beings, who were looked upon as more fortunate and blessed than their companions.

The night had afforded but one pleasure, one rich reward, for the labors of the day; this was to sleep and dream. But, the idleness of the early evening hours, when the mind was keenly active and speculation unlimited, became the dread of each day. Surely life held something better than this, even though the light of the sun and the shadows of the night painted no picture of an answer to the mystery.

Then came the discovery of the spark, the light, the flame, the fire, the heat! In an instant, the life of primitive man and woman was changed. The darkness of the night could be dispelled, the coldness of the evening air and morning breeze could be modified, metals could be reduced to malleable forms, and food could be prepared more tastefully than in the past.

The greatest change of all, however, was that which came with the coming of *light*. Light at night. Light in the darkest hours and in the darkest home. Light and warmth at the fireside. A hearthplace of comfort. A place where the long and silent hours of the night might be profitably spent. Pleasure, comfort, discourse, learning!

The coming of the night was anticipated with joy throughout the day. When the setting sun brought an end to the hunt and to the work of the fields, and when the tired body could no longer carry on, there were still the hours of the evening to refresh man and afford him the luxurious pleasure of warmth while he rested in enjoyable companionship before the fire.

Sitting in the glowing lights of the blessed fire, the mind was tricked into concentration upon the fantastic forms and weird action of the flames. The marvels of nature's powers and possibilities intrigued the imagination and tempted the speculative faculties of primitive man's receptive consciousness. Here, meditation was the school, and the mysteries of life the teacher who questioned and drew forth the answer from the inspired impressions of each mind.

To this fiery shrine came others with their questions, their dreams, their problems, and their desire for light *and more light.* The fireplace became the center of the temple of mystery, and the hearthstone became the altar of the worship of primitive man, when his thoughts were turned toward nature and its marvels.

It was here that men first directed their thoughts toward the possibility of an omnipotent power which ruled the forces of the universe and created the bounties of life; it was here that primitive men first lifted their thoughts beyond themselves to that which must be greater than the greatest among them. It was here that men first sought the castles of the soul, more grand than the castles of the body or the castles they built with mud and wood.

Heathens they were called, because they worshiped at the hearthstone. Castles they sought, for in castles there were protection, warmth, comfort, and the time to think and dream. Mansions of the souls they looked for and found at last in the uplift of their thoughts and the uniting of their minds in one perfect conception of a heavenly realm.

Still, there was always the quest for knowledge and the desire for answers to problems unsolved. "Why are we here? who are we? whence came we? and whither do we go?" There were the questions that were asked at the first hearthstone, and are asked today at every hearthstone, with the same sincerity and an increasing desire for explicit and understandable explanations.

Have we, as individuals, a definite mission in life? Is each human being an entity, an individuality, known to and considered by the Infinite Intelligence as an important element in the universal scheme of things? Is the earth, after all, merely a stage, presenting a passing drama into which we have cast ourselves by our own voluntary preference? And when our parts are played, is our work on earth truly done?

The sacred scriptures of all religions speak of only one earth, one globe, one place in the whole of the universe where man was created and exists as an image of some Creator. Science, on the other hand, busily occupies itself on the borderline of discovery, anticipating that it may reveal to us at any moment the actual existence of other planets than this one, filled with human life or living creatures not unlike ourselves. The gospels of the ages and of all nations speak of great avatars and messengers of the Holy Messiah and the God of Gods, who have come to earth to save all living beings. Is there no redemption, no saving grace, for the beings on other planets, or have they no souls, no personalities that are divine and worthy of infinite consideration?

Is this personality of ours, this individuality which we strive to build up through idealism and the elimination of undesirable traits, merely a temporary or imaginary creation of our minds?

Down through the ages has come the cry for *light* and *more light.* About us, everything is changing and nothing seems permanent and fixed. The mountains crumble away, the rivers dry up and cease to flow, islands sink, and new seas are formed. The great oaks, in all their majesty, must succumb to transition, to change, or death. Man goes on his way and crosses the borderline into the unknown and seems to end his existence in the twinkling of an eye. Is there any part of man, therefore, or any part of nature, that is immortal, unchanging, permanent, and continuous?

Is there a survival beyond man's mere memory of the personalities that now exist in human form? Will the death of the body or the change of its form release an intangible and invisible something that will rise to greater heights than the monuments to remembered characters, or surmount the limitations of time and space, and thereby attain incorruptibility and immortality?

If the present physical body is a mansion of the soul and the Great Messenger of God went forward to prepare other places of this soul, are there other mansions then to be attained, and how?

It has been the hope of the world—and the inspiring power that has enabled man to carry on in the face of mighty obstacles—that some day he would be freed of the mortal cloak that enslaves him on this earth and he would rise to a life of eternal bliss and goodness. If the religions that have inspired man are true, and the culminating joy of his life is to be found only in the spiritual existence of his soul in a realm beyond the earth, why have the souls of millions been imprisoned here to suffer and to know torment, sorrow, strife, and conflict? What end is served, what mission fulfilled, by the incarnation of the soul here? If, out of the sublime, spiritual consciousness of a blissful kingdom comes each soul, and to this same high state must it return to enjoy its divine heritage, why is it sent forth from such a transcendental place to dwell in association with corruption, sin, evil, and dross?

These are the questions which millions are asking today and which must be answered more completely, more satisfyingly, and more constructively than they have been answered in the past. Directing our attention to the worship of God, and inspiring us with the belief that this God is loving, merciful, tender, and just, will not answer these questions but will merely add to the mystery of our existence. Granted that an omnipotent, all-wise, merciful, and loving God created us in his image and directed into these physical bodies a part of his soul consciousness to suffer and to endure the trials and tribulations of unknown and unexpected experiences here on earth, still the question remains, "Why are we here?" and "How are mercy, love, and justice made manifest in such a plan?"

CHAPTER 2

WHY ARE WE HERE?

To those who say, "I do not believe in the doctrine of rebirth or immortality," I would like to reply by saying, "Do you really know what the doctrine actually means?"

In twenty years of public lecturing and writing on subjects dealing with spiritual and cosmic principles, I have found thousands who were ready to express strongly their disbelief in certain doctrines, and yet had to admit that they neither understood them nor had ever attempted to investigate them. It is truly difficult for one to accept a doctrine that is not understood, and it is especially difficult to accept a doctrine or principle that has been popularly misrepresented. This tendency on the part of human nature is nothing new, for in the time of Jesus, and for centuries preceding his introduction of new principles, the races of man rejected many doctrines which they did not properly comprehend.

No one compliments himself by saying that he has discarded or rejected a statement, a principle, or a law that he neither understands nor gives sufficient consideration to comprehend. Such an attitude is one of intolerance, bigotry, or ignorance. One may appear to be with the majority or with the popular mind in smiling at new ideas or new principles, but, after all, the smile may have to be changed tomorrow by the sudden discovery on the part of the populace that the rejected or ridiculed idea has been found true and acceptable.

After all, what is there about the real doctrine of human rebirth that any strictly orthodox religious person, or any rigidly scientific mind, cannot accept? I will grant you that there are certain things about the popular notions of reincarnation that are absurd and so greatly misrepresented that the logically minded or thinking person feels that it is a presumption upon his intelligence even to consider the statements made. When, however, we find that three fourths of the world's thinking and analyzing minds have accepted a certain principle or doctrine for many ages, and when we find that the best-informed persons and the keenest intellects in the business, scientific, and religious world have given their approval and credence to such a doctrine or principle, then we should feel inclined to give a few minutes' thought to the doctrine and discover whether there is in it the essence of truth or probability. This is only fair to ourselves and fair to the doctrine.

We have learned through experience in the past century that the popular impression of a doctrine, principle, or idea may be very wrong. We have learned through many important examples that even the learned persons and the commentators in encyclopedias may be misinformed in regard to certain principles and thereby influence or prejudice our understanding. Certainly, we in the Western world have learned that popular criticism is not always a standard by which we may safely gauge our own convictions.

All of this is particularly true regarding the subject of human rebirth. When we read in the question-and-answer columns of the largest newspapers in America that a clergy-man, who is nationally known and is devoting his time principally to the answering of religious questions, states that his understanding of this doctrine is that man may be born again as a cat or a dog, or some other animal lower in the scale than the human being, we keenly realize what an injustice is being done to a very beautiful and important law of nature through gross ignorance or wilful misunderstanding. And, if such a learned man has no better understanding of the real principles of reincarnation than this, we should not be surprised that lesser lights, or those millions who do not have access to sources of information, should have other distorted ideas regarding reincarnation.

Perhaps the most important point to be kept in mind by each investigator on this subject is that the doctrine or law of reincarnation is not a religious creed, a religious doctrine, or a religious law. It is a natural law and has to do with the evolution of nature and the carrying out of nature's principles aside from any connection these principles may have with the revelation of God and God's omnipotent intelligence. In other words, the laws pertaining to reincarnation are no more religious than are the laws pertaining to conception, the growth of the embryo, and the birth of the body. God's divine laws as natural laws are unquestionably operating in this marvelous process of the reproduction of the human race, but no one would classify the study of embryology as a religious doctrine or a religious creed. The facts pertaining to embryology are strictly within the domain of science. Likewise, no one would think of classifying the study of disease, the breaking down of the human body and its ultimate transition, as a religious or theological study, even though divine principles are involved.

Furthermore, a careful and truly conscientious study of the doctrine of reincarnation reveals that there is nothing in the true principles that may be considered contradictory to any of the religious principles found in any of the recognized or long-established religions. Reincarnation in its truthful presentation is not antagonistic toward the principles of sound theology, and I know that Christians will be astonished when I say that there is nothing in the truthful presentation of the doctrine of reincarnation that is contrary to, or inconsistent with, the fundamental Christian principles *as revealed and taught by Jesus.* A reading of the other chapters of this book will prove that this is so, and it is a notable fact in the Western world today that Christians find more joy in the true understanding of the doctrine of reincarnation than do persons of other denominations. The reason for this will become apparent as this book is read. Again I say, however, that some of the popular notions regarding reincarnation and some of the wilfully misrepresented fancies connected therewith are not only inconsistent with the Christian theology and doctrine, but with all true religions.

One of the most often repeated criticisms of the doctrine of reincarnation, generally expressed by those who have had only a casual understanding of it, is to the effect that it seems strange that God should require the soul of man to have many and varied experiences here on earth. Persons expressing this idea generally say that they cannot see why the soul of man could not continue to exist without requiring incarnation in a physical body on this earth plane. This argument is generally presented as a conclusive and final closing of the entire discussion. However, such an argument is fundamentally unsound. It is not based upon any rational premise. The fact of the matter is that the doctrine of reincarnation does not start with the assumption, or the theory, that man *must be* incarnated in a physical body and have earthly experiences. Reincarnation starts with the fact that man *is* incarnated in a physical body and *is* here having earthly experiences. Since these two wonderful facts are established by our actual existence here, and are, therefore, removed from the field of speculation and are not mere assumptions used in the doctrine of reincarnation, we must begin with the fact that man *is* here and *is* living in a physical body, and confine ourselves to answering the question of "Why?"

Since the dawn of civilization, when man began to think of his vicissitudes, trials, and tribulations, and to seek for some reward for all that he suffered, he has asked the same question over and over, "Why are we here?" Theology has its answer to this question and the answer has become evolved and involved until it is no longer a brief, definite statement, but a group of statements constituting a creed; and there are many creeds according to the various viewpoints and beliefs. Science, on the other hand, has its answer also. But the scientific answer does not cover all of the elements, all of the principles which concern man more deeply than do the problems of cosmology and biology.

If one eliminates the religious elements of the question, "Why are we here?" and confines the discussion to either the materialistic or the atheistic viewpoint, there is still a great need for more light and more information on the complex problems included in the question.

It is not sufficient, either, to say that we are here because of some divine principle known only to God and incomprehensible to man. There is nothing in the whole history of civilization and in the cultural development of man to indicate that any of the laws of nature or any of the laws of God were ever intended to be concealed and kept from man's understanding. The very inner nature of man seems to be inspired with an unquenchable thirst for knowledge about himself and his relationship to the universe, and nothing short of the truth in these matters will suffice. Our encyclopedias and textbooks of knowledge are filled today with free and exhaustive explanations of laws and principles which were at one time or another proclaimed to be God's secret knowledge, and beyond the comprehension of man's finite mind. Those very questions, which at one time were condemned by church and state as heretical and beyond the right or privilege of man to ask, are now freely asked and answered with precise knowledge by both church and state institutions. In fact, religious and educational foundations are active today in the promulgation of knowledge pertaining to those very things which were condemned by the church at one time as nobody's business and God's secret prerogatives.

Since we *are here*, and since the church, through its theologies, claims that we are here because God created us to live on this earth plane, we have a right to ask the *why* and the *wherefore*. And, since science also claims that our existence here is in accordance with a definite law of evolution which is a logical consequence of the divine, creative principle, we have a right to ask science to investigate still further and tell us what purpose is served by our existence.

This book, then, is an attempt to explain in non-technical language, and without religious bias or prejudice, the reason for the incarnation of a *divine soul* in a *physical body,* and the purpose or mission of that soul in a physical body on this earth plane. The explanation does not involve any propaganda for a new religion, a new creed, or a new form of worship. It does not attempt to soothe the weariness and struggles of life, nor blunt our minds to the obligations of life. That the doctrine of reincarnation does bring, in its understanding, a newer and different viewpoint of life resulting in more contentment and more harmonious cooperation with nature's laws is simply in the nature of the laws revealed. But that newer viewpoint and that contentment which comes with the understanding of the doctrine of reincarnation in no way lessens the seriousness of life or makes man immune to the sufferings and tribulations which he must endure.

Finally, I may add without seeming to be facetious, that whether one believes in or accepts the doctrine of reincarnation or rejects it, the truth of its principles will continue to manifest itself and the laws will continue to operate. We neither obliterate nor modify a law or principle by denying it or refusing to accept it. Therefore, it behooves everyone to become acquainted with the facts and at least to know something of the laws under which we are living and by which we are directed and controlled in our existence.

We may continue to live without knowing these things, and we may find some degree of satisfaction in life without understanding any of the principles involved. The whole culture and advancement of man's civilization, however, has proved that man has become more happy, more contented, and more masterful through understanding every natural and divine law involved in his existence. The constant quest for more knowledge along these lines indicates the restlessness of man's nature because of his determination to gain greater success and joy in life through the knowledge that is necessary for him to possess. For this reason, the knowledge of the doctrine of reincarnation will constitute one of the most beneficial aids to his education.

CHAPTER 3

THE ANCIENT BELIEFS

The one incontestable fact which is the foundation of our whole study of man's existence is that man is here on earth and that his life consists of a series of experiences which at various periods bring joy and sorrow, happiness and sadness, contentment and unrest, love and hatred, peace and suffering.

The second important fact revealed through the experiences of life is that man's nature is dual, or at least it is dual in manifestation. He is a physical, mortal body, with humanly conceived ideas and ideals, desires, ambitions, and conceptions. He is also an emotional or spiritual body having a subjective self or consciousness, which urges submission to its desires, inspirations, tendencies, and inclinations. Between these two sides of man's nature there is a constant contest for supremacy and domination. Hence, man has come to think of himself as being more than a mere physical body like a mass of matter united by a chemical formula, and more than a mere mechanical contrivance like an automaton. He is likewise convinced by the sufferings and ordeals of the flesh that he is more than a purely spiritual being.

In attempting to find an answer to the question: "Why are we here?" man cannot subdue or cast out of his consciousness the idea that if he could determine *what* he is, he would know *why* he is. Therefore, along with man's quest for knowledge concerning the purpose of his existence in an earthly life is the desire for knowledge concerning himself and his relation to the universe.

Theology has always attempted to explain what man is and why he was created. Science begins its explanation of man's nature at a point where man is already a living, thinking entity. It does not deal with those phases of his creation that precede the chemical, the biological, or the mechanical constitution of his nature and being. This pre-entity period of man's creation has been left to theology to explain. The theological answers have been varied and unique in accordance with the periods of time through which man has passed in the process of civilization, and in accordance with the light of knowledge possessed by the nations in all ages from antiquity to the present moment.

There is one point of agreement to be found, however, in all of the theological explanations offered in regard to the nature of man's being. In all times and among all races, and in all degrees of cultural education, the inspired or logically evolved answer has been that man is a physical body with its accompanying physical consciousness, in which resides a soul, or a divine self, or a segment of some divine consciousness constituting an inner self. The duality of man's existence is, therefore, a universally accepted idea. That idea is challenged by science since it cannot accept as a fact any premise or any principle beyond its ken. In all religions, however, the idea of an inner man or inner self is a fundamental which is stated as neither theory nor speculative conclusion.

If one denies the existence of an inner consciousness or soul as an entity distinct and apart from the physical body, then the whole subject of birth and rebirth reduces itself to a consideration of chemical action and reaction, and its purely physical principles. Such a belief would preclude any consideration of the subject of reincarnation just as it would preclude any consideration of the immortality of any part of man or the existence of any divine element in man. Therefore, since we are not dealing with the materialistic and non-divine idea of man's being, we must set aside this phase of speculation and adopt the more universal idea that man is a physical body clothing a soul or form of spiritual consciousness.

Looking upon man, therefore, as a dual being, body and soul, we are forced to turn to theology and the religious doctrines of the past and present to find any illumination regarding the immaterial part of man. The scientist says that we may look to him for any and every explanation pertaining to the chemical, biological, pathological, and physiological nature of man's existence. We must turn to ontology and theology for our knowledge regarding the spiritual part of man. Whether the present-day scientist is right in thus limiting his field of investigation, or is wrong in this regard, we may determine after we have studied the question in the future chapters of this book. We may say in passing, however, that it was not always so. Theology was not always a subject of study apart from the general philosophical sciences. Nor was there always a distinct study known as the *sciences* as we have it today. Nor was there always a time when man, in his search for truth about himself, found two opposed schools dealing with distinct dual parts of his nature.

However, the tendency in modern times has been to leave all questions pertaining to the spiritual or infinite consciousness of man to the schools of theology, and if we are to accept any of their explanations in regard to the nature of man and his relation to the universe, we must enter into a simple summary of them, for they are too diverse, contradictory, and inconsistent to serve any purpose through elaborate examination of their minute details.

In brief, we find theology in general throughout the ages admitting one fact or claiming one point with consistency. It is to the effect that the real part of man is the infinite, divine, or intangible consciousness and essence which constitutes the inner self. For this inner self many names have been invented and universally adopted at various times. The most general of these names is that of *soul,* and we find it associated with another word, which means the *breath;* and for many ages the inner self of man was associated with the idea of breathing an invisible essence which constituted the spiritual nature of man. A second general principle most universally and consistently adopted was the idea that this soul of man is a distinct entity, or a spiritual something, that is immortal and at times separates from the physical body.

Thus we have two important points coming down to us from antiquity as fundamental principles involved in the explanation of man's spiritual existence. These points we find beautifully incorporated in an attempt to explain the creation of man in the translated book of Genesis in the modern Christian Bible. Therein, we read that God made man out of the dust of the earth which represented the physical, chemical, mechanical, and material part of his being, and into this God breathed as a second part of man the breath, or essence, or consciousness, of life, and the physical body became a living, or animated, visible soul.

Two important secondary principles are intimated by this symbolical or allegorical process of man's creation. First, that the physical body, made of the material elements of the earth, was completed and perfected as a purely material form before any consideration was given to the process of animating it with consciousness of life. Second, that with the physical body completed and yet lifeless, it was necessary for something more to be done to make it a living being, and that to do this there was added a second and a distinctly different and separate element called "the breath of life." After this entered the physical body, the physical part became insignificant, for man was then not merely an animated body, or a physical body that was filled with life, but a *soul* that could live on earth and manifest itself and was, therefore, *a living soul.*

When the original version of this passage in the Bible is read and analyzed in its original tongue, one is more deeply impressed with the significance of the second point. We are impressed with the fact that the physical body did not take on life but that the invisible, infinite *soul* took on a physical form by the uniting of the breath with the body. Even the ancients were impressed with this significance, and in their philosophies, which gradually evolved into theological principles, we are constantly reminded of the fact that man is essentially a *soul* clothed with a body, and not a body animated with a soul.

A further survey of the theological and philosophical explanations of the past and the present reveals some other points consistently adhered to in the explanations, though often modified in accordance with sectarian creeds. These are to the effect that the breath of life, or soul of man, was originally a part of the Creator, or God essence and consciousness. We are reminded in many ways and by many words that whereas the physical part of man is an accumulation of unorganized elements gathered together from the products of the earth, the *soul* of man is something that was drawn out of space and made into a form to be placed in man. We are reminded also that whereas the physical part of man was made out of nothing that had any form or nature of man in it, the soul of man already existed in the soul and consciousness of the Creator when he made the body of man.

We are reminded also by other points of the explanations that the soul in man existed from the beginning of all time and must continue to exist until the end of time, if there be such an end. In most of the philosophical explanations we are impressed with the belief that the soul's immortality distinctly implied that since it was not mortal and could have no end, it never had any beginning, whereas man's physical body had a distinct beginning when it was created out of the lesser and unorganized elements of the earth, and would have an ending when these mortal elements lost their organization and became disassociated.

Finally, our survey of the theological and philosophical explanations of the spiritual part of man reveals a universal belief in the principle that the soul or consciousness of man was always a part of the soul of the Creator, or God, and that it will live, or exist, or continue to function, as long as God or the Creator exists.

In these principles and ideas, therefore, we have a very definite picture of the nature of man's being. We have man as a physical being represented by his physical body composed of the material elements of the earth. Within this physical body we have the spiritual body or soul. Man is therefore dual, body and soul. His body is mortal, being composed of mortal elements or of corruption, to use a theological term. Its mortality makes it corruptible. The spiritual part of man, or the soul essence, is a part of the God consciousness, and is infinite, divine, and immortal. It was originally, and is essentially in its nature, of the immortal and incorruptible. It resides in the body of man and, therefore, takes on a cloak of corruption, for the body of man cannot always continue, but must decay and corrupt.

The soul is therefore only temporarily resident within a physical body and cannot remain eternally in one body, since in that case the body would have to be immortal, as is the soul. Man is born with a new body recently composed of the chemical elements of the earth, and into this enters the pure and immortal soul that has always existed and will continue to exist for all eternity. The mortality and corruptibility of the body cannot affect the immortality and incorruptibility of the soul. Therefore, there must come a time when the physical body in its corruption becomes disorganized and can no longer contain the soul essence. A change takes place which is incorrectly called *death*, but which is merely a transition. Body and soul are separated and the corruptible goes into corruption, and the immortal and incorruptible retains its infinite state.

Science has proved the correctness of the belief in the mortality and corruption of the physical body. The experiences of the flesh in our individual lives demonstrate that from hour to hour, and from day to day, we rebuild our physical bodies with the material elements of the earth in order to replace the corruptible and worn-out elements which previously composed it. Our other experiments have shown that the physical body can completely wear out and become so incapable of retaining life and vitality that the so-called breath of life, or soul consciousness, leaves it.

By these experiences of science and our individual lives, we become convinced that it is a part of the economy of the Creator's laws, and of the economy of life itself, for the soul to separate itself from the corrupting and corruptible physical body and leave the body to continue its transition into primary elements again, by which it returns to the dust of the earth, while the soul remains immortal.

If this broad and general explanation of the nature of man's being is acceptable to you, my reader, then you are face to face with the next important question: "Why is the soul of God, or the Creator's consciousness, placed temporarily in a *physical* body, and what becomes of it after its release?" That double question has been the most insistent and most important query in the consciousness of man since the dawn of thinking and believing. It is to answer that question with more facts and less theory that this book was written and dedicated to thinking men and women.

CHAPTER 4

THE QUEST

I have intimated that one of the objections on the part of those who are fundamentalists of the modern type in their religious viewpoints is that the doctrine of rebirth seems to place the soul of man in the position of being a *spiritual entity,* continuously bound to *earthly* conditions. Such persons say that it is disturbing to the peace of their minds and their spirits to think of the soul as requiring earthly experiences, trials, and tribulations in order to evolve or perfect itself. They also argue that it should not be necessary for the soul to have earthly experience or to require any process or system of earthly development. Their contention is that the soul of man is a divine, infinite, spiritual something, having its origin in God and maintaining eternally its transcendental nature, and that it can be neither added to nor subtracted from, nor in any way made more divine than it is when it leaves God and enters the body of man. A final contention is that it is horrifying to think that the soul must have more than one contact with the quagmire of earthly contamination instead of returning to the eternal spiritual world and remaining there in its sublime spiritual state.

All of these arguments are based upon certain assumptions which are faulty, or at least misunderstood. In the first place, attention is called to the fact that the soul of man *is* here in a physical body and *is* in contact with the earthly experiences, and this fact is neither an assumption nor a simple matter of doctrinal faith. All of our reasoning and arguing about the why and wherefore of the soul's incarnation in a physical body here on this plane cannot alter the fact that *it is here* and is passing through a process of experiences.

Granting that the soul in its spiritual essence is absolutely perfect and sublime and that no earthly experiences can improve this high degree of perfection, and granting that the soul has its origin in the consciousness of God but is nevertheless infused in a physical body to live for a time on this earth plane, we come face to face with the question as to why a soul in its perfection should require earthly experiences for even a day or an hour.

Orthodox theology of the Western world briefly and simply says that there is a divine reason and purpose for the soul's contact with earthly conditions and its incarnation for a time in a physical body on this earth plane. That is really saying something that common sense would admit. It is not a theological conclusion but a rational conclusion. We cannot possibly conceive of there being no reason, no purpose, and no great end to be served by the incarnation of the soul in a physical body. To think of such an important element in the scheme of things as being purposeless would be to tear away the very foundation of our faith in the belief that the whole universe and everything in it exists and operates in accordance with law and reason, and that God has established nothing or instituted nothing that did not have some definite purpose or plan back of its motive and existence.

It is my purpose in this book to show that there is a good reason, a logical reason, and an acceptable reason for the soul's incarnation in the physical body. This reason is not contrary to any of the sound, theological principles, and fortunately it is consistent with the understanding held by all of the religious movements of the world. By understanding these reasons and analyzing them, even casually, one is better prepared to understand the real purpose of our existence here on earth and to see why the true doctrines of reincarnation—freed from all of the unsound idiosyncrasies that personal opinion has attached to them—are plausible and acceptable to the thinking mind.

Starting then with the fact that the soul in its essence and vital nature is a spiritual substance originating in the consciousness of God and emanating from the spiritual realm, we proceed to study the attributes of this soul and learn what it really is, and why it may benefit by contact with earthly experiences.

Perhaps only in the Western world and among Western religions is the nature of the soul so little understood. The rapid advance and propagation of the claims of modern spiritualism represents a form of speculation possible only because of the lack of knowledge on the part of persons in the Western world regarding the soul, its nature, and its attributes. To the Orientals and to almost three fourths of the world's religious population the many preposterous claims of spiritualism as a religion, a philosophy, or a popular belief originated in the Western world solely because of popular misconception regarding the soul. It was claimed recently by one eminent clergyman, who regretted the increasing interest in spiritualistic seances in America, that the World War [I] with the attendant loss of millions of lives was responsible for the great increase in numbers of persons who turned to spiritualism to find some consolation, and perhaps some illumination, in regard to the unknown or sudden passing of beloved ones. But in many foreign nations there was also a tremendous loss of life, and among these peoples there was not the frantic turning to spiritualism for understanding because most of these foreign persons were too well acquainted with certain fundamental facts which enabled them to understand what the Western minds had not yet learned.

Clergymen in the Western world are as responsible as any others for the progress of spiritualism, for if the churches of the Western world and the religions of the Occidental had not eliminated from their early doctrines and creeds the principles which revealed the true nature and attributes of the soul, there would not be the present-day misunderstanding and misconception in this regard, and the many mystical movements now found in America and England would have no actual necessity as a foundation for their existence.

In most of Europe, and in all of America, the great fundamental truths of man's spiritual nature and existence have been modified or entirely eliminated from modern creeds and dogmas. If these were understood as well today as they were in the days when Jesus the Christ talked to his disciples and with the multitudes, and when the foundation for the Christian church was laid, there would be no need for any such book as the present one or the hundreds of others which have been published within the last ten years casting new light on the teachings of Jesus, and the pristine principles of Christianity.

CHAPTER 5

THE COSMIC CONCEPTION
OF THE SOUL

In the Occidental or Western world there is a general or popular idea of the soul which pictures it as an invisible, intangible, spiritual substance of an immortal nature. This substance is believed to be the "breath of life," or, in other words, an etheric vitality emanating from the Source of All Sources and carrying with it the creative power or energy of the Creator of all things that exist. In brief, it is believed to be a spiritual essence, the nature of which is to give animation and life to all conscious things.

This is all that can be definitely stated by the most orthodox and enthusiastic followers of the religions of the Western world.

We may divide the principal religious denominations of the Western world into two broad classifications under the headings of Jewish and Christian. Therefore, let us pause just a moment to see what the leading authorities in those two fields of religious thought have to say regarding the soul. Turning first to the *Jewish Encyclopedia,* we find that the nature of the soul, as taught in the Talmud, is that which was conceived by Philo, the philosopher. This conception— which is a human conception—is that the soul is dual in nature. One part is called the *active soul*, which is the consciousness breathed by God into man, and the other part is the *vital spirit* with which he inspired man. Here we have the foundation for a distinction between spirit and soul, as two parts of the same thing, and a reason for the confusion in regard to spirit and soul, which leads many modern religious writers and preachers to use the two terms synonymously as though they were identical. It is this confusion which is responsible for the spiritualistic movement and similar movements using the term *spirit* for the term *soul*. We note in the *Jewish Encyclopedia* also that in some prayers the phrase is used, "May God give spirit and soul to the embryo." In other Jewish writings, quoted in the encyclopedia, it appears that the Jews believed that all souls are preexistent and that there are souls of different quality. The rabbis, according to the encyclopedia, do not agree in the belief of the preexistence of the soul. According to them "each and every soul which shall be from Adam until the end of the world, was formed during the six days of creation and was in Paradise."

For the Christian viewpoint, we may turn to the original Christian doctrines, as presented in the *Catholic Encyclopedia*. Here, we read that the soul "may be defined as the ultimate, internal principle by which we think, feel, and will, and by which our bodies are animated." In this expression we find the Christian idea that in addition to the vitality which animates the physical body through the coming of the soul, there is a form of consciousness or mind that accompanies the soul and which enables this physical body to see, to think, and feel, and act with understanding.

Much more is said in both of these encyclopedias about the soul. Many peculiar ideas are expressed therein which will probably surprise and astonish the average devoted Jew and Christian. Further presentation and discussions of these unusual ideas regarding the soul will be referred to in other parts of this book in connection with the points raised by them. At the present moment we are concerned solely with the nature of the soul and not its origin or the means of its entrance into the body or its purpose after it has become incarnated.

We note, therefore, that the Jewish and Christian religions adopted the almost universal idea of all other religions claiming that the soul of man was not only a vitalizing essence of a divine nature but the *seat* of consciousness or mind. We may safely say, therefore, that the universal human conception of the soul today is that it is the vitality and consciousness in man. This must be the view of every orthodox Christian and every orthodox Jew of the Western world, as well as the conviction of every orthodox person of the various religions throughout the Oriental world. With such a general foundation for an analysis of the soul and its nature, let us turn to the viewpoint as expressed by mystical revelation and see what is the cosmic conception of the soul.

First, we discover that there is a very definite distinction between spirit and soul. Spirit is the animating vitality or energy that permeates all living matter in the universe. We must remind the reader right here that it is unnecessary to use the term *living matter*, since all matter is *living*. There is a difference between living matter and conscious matter. Rocks are living in the sense that there is a vitality, or force, or energy which infuses every crystal and every atom of their structure, and which holds the mass together in the proper atomic and molecular form to express the specific nature of matter. All matter is vibrant with this universal energy or essence which is universally called *spirit*. It is in every cell of the elements composing the body of man, the body of every plant and vegetable, and of every material thing in definite expression in the universe. Spirit is, therefore, the universal essence that creates and maintains the expression of matter. Chemically speaking, or from the viewpoint of physics, we may say that the essence which composes the electron is the universal spirit. Therefore, we will put the subject of spirit aside for a moment and consider soul as something apart from spirit.

Our cosmic conception shows us that the soul of man and all conscious creatures is a form of divine consciousness, which has certain attributes or functions. It may, therefore, be called *infinite mind.* This infinite mind has certain faculties which we may term *seeing, feeling, hearing, smelling* and *tasting.* These faculties are not separate and distinct functionings, as they are in the physical body, but a group or amalgamated faculty of apprehension and comprehension which in any one of its five forms of impression or receptivity is interpreted by us as that of seeing, feeling, tasting, hearing, or smelling. In other words, the mind of the soul is capable of receiving and comprehending knowledge through a faculty of perception, which is a combination of seeing, hearing, feeling, tasting, and smelling. The reception and interpretation of an impression by the soul is translated to our outer physical consciousness in the terms of the senses: seeing, feeling, hearing, tasting, or smelling. Judging the soul impressions, then, from our objective or physical form of consciousness, we would feel at times as though the soul had seen something, or heard something, or felt something, whereas, as a matter of fact, the soul impression was not through any limited channel of one means of consciousness.

The perception or reception of knowledge or impression by the soul through its one complex channel constitutes what modern mystics term the *psychic sense*. When this sense receives an impression which is prophetic, it is called *intuition*. By others the psychic sense is called the channel for inspiration. Many other terms are used to describe this perceptive and comprehending faculty of the soul, and among the Oriental religions and philosophies we find many strange words indicating the rather indefinite idea I have attempted to express in the foregoing sentences.

Thus, the soul has the attribute of comprehension, as a faculty of its consciousness. It has likewise the faculty of communicating, through a similar channel of psychic impressions, the thoughts within its consciousness. These thoughts impress themselves on the consciousness of the soul in other physical bodies by a simple process. The soul in man, being a part of the God consciousness or Oversoul of the universe, is never separated from the soul that is resident in every physical body, and a thought in the consciousness of the soul in one physical body can be immediately in contact with the consciousness in the soul of any other, or every other, physical body on the earth plane or in the spiritual realm.

Right here we have a cosmic truth which, if developed to its full explanation and understanding, would make plain the misconceptions of the modern spiritualistic doctrines. Nothing said in the foregoing paragraphs is consistent with nor in support of any of the claims made by the spiritualistic doctrines of the present day. In fact, an understanding of these cosmic truths will reveal the error of the present-day spiritualistic beliefs and practices, and will make plain why many comprehensible experiences and revelations have come spontaneously and unexpectedly through what has seemed to be an application of the spiritualistic principles.

This mind of the consciousness in the soul, being part of the Infinite Mind, is wise in all universal cosmic wisdom. This does not mean, however, that the essential wisdom of the soul, which it possessed before it ever became incarnated in a physical body, includes a knowledge of all of man's artificially established and arbitrarily created beliefs and practices. It is often argued by the young student of mysticism and metaphysics that since the soul is infinite in its wisdom, there can be no reason for the statement that through its experiences here on earth it adds to its knowledge, and if it possesses all knowledge, it cannot possibly add to that wisdom.

Such students overlook the fact that the infinite mind of the soul previous to any incarnation on this earth plane would not be familiar with such mundane knowledge as the Sanskrit alphabet, the Morse code, the invented laws of man's form of chemistry, the driving of an automobile, the best methods to use in buying and selling in the stock market, or the ethical codes and legal statutes arbitrarily established by man in various countries, communities, and localities. The universal wisdom possessed by the soul before incarnation and ever afterwards retained as its fundamental knowledge pertains strictly to cosmic laws and principles—divine decrees and rulings.

When we stop to consider that the essential knowledge of one nation in one part of the world today is not the essential knowledge of another nation in another part of the world, or of the same nation in that part of the world centuries ago, we will realize that human knowledge, or earthly knowledge of human origin and application, is a transient, mortal something that changes rapidly and is not fixed for all times. The soul would not be aided in its earthly purposes during its incarnation in a body by being conscious of all the human knowledge accumulated by it through all ages.

The essential knowledge possessed by the infinite mind of the soul is that transcendental knowledge which man cannot obtain through any of the human channels or through any of the physical organs of perception and which he must, therefore, obtain through a spiritual means.

The coming of the soul into the body, therefore, is not for a single purpose, and we realize at once that we now have two good reasons for the incarnation of a spiritual soul in a human body. First, that for a reason which we will explain shortly, the soul is to have certain earthly experiences, and secondly, the human physical body is to have the advantage of spiritual knowledge and illumination in addition to its mundane knowledge.

The next point for our consideration is that after the soul is incarnated in the physical body and brings to the physical body the divine consciousness and wisdom, plus the transcendental faculty of perception and communication with the soul consciousness of the universe, we have a combination which in the human form expresses the closest approximation to the image of God.

Even a cursory examination of the principles of biology, anatomy, and pathology indicates to us that the physical body of man, independent of the soul and its consciousness, has a form of consciousness and intelligence of its own. The most minute biological cell under examination through the microscope reveals reactions to light, color, and heat, and other external conditions, which prove that it has a primitive form of consciousness of its own. This physical, mundane consciousness is limited and mortal. The smallest living organisms, such as the smallest ones living in water, are an aggregate of the primitive cells, and their bodies contain, therefore, the aggregate consciousness of the cells that compose the bodies. The physical consciousness in each living body on the face of the earth is no more than the aggregate consciousness of the cells composing the body.

Limiting our discussion to man's physical body, we note from scientific experiments that the consciousness in the cells which compose the roots of our hair is a different consciousness from that which is in the cells composing the fingernails, the bones, the outer tissues, the muscles, the blood, or the other parts of our bodies. Each cell carries on its functioning and adjusts itself to its environment with similar cells and maintains its personality and integrity, its individuality, and its usefulness in accordance with the distinct consciousness within it. The cells which produce hair would not produce bone or tissue, or any other form of matter. No matter where they may congregate or with what other cells they may associate, they will strive against great odds and under very adverse conditions to maintain and perpetuate, establish and reproduce, their individual nature in accordance with their individual consciousness. There are forms of physical disorders in the human body where hair cells, teeth cells, bone cells, and others, accumulate in an unnatural position or relationship and continue to manifest their natures and reproduce that which they were intended to reproduce, despite the obstacle of wrong environment and abnormal situations.

The consciousness of the physical body is, therefore, an aggregation of the consciousness in every physical cell of the human body, and is likewise a combination of the different natures of consciousness of the many kinds of cells.

The mystic knows, therefore, that the difference between the most highly evolved ape and even the primitive man is not a question of soul evolution but a question of the difference between the natures of consciousness in the cells composing the physical body and the dwelling of a human soul in that body instead of the soul of an ape. In other words, the difference between the ape and the human is not only a difference of the soul in each of them but a difference also of the aggregate and combined consciousness of the cells which compose the physical bodies of each. An ape, therefore, could not evolve into a man by suddenly having a soul of man enter its physical body in place of the soul of an ape. A great change would have to be made in the physical consciousness of its body as well.

Nor could the ape become a man by any process of evolution whereby the physical consciousness in the cells of the body of the ape became like unto the consciousness in the physical body of man, unless at the same time a human soul entered the body of an ape. The idea of seeking, therefore, for a single missing link in the evolutionary stage of cell life composing the physical body of the ape is a foolish one. The greater missing link in such an imaginary chain would be the single link representing the stage of change from the soul of an ape to the soul of man. And no one can seriously consider making a search for such a link.

Man's physical body, therefore, has a consciousness distinctly its own, limited and adjusted through attunement of its faculties to perceive and comprehend things of its own nature. The consciousness of physical man is keenly attuned to the consciousness of all physical nature. But it cannot be attuned to the consciousness of the Cosmic or Divine Mind, for this is of a transcendental nature and of a higher vibratory rate than the vibrations of the physical consciousness. All of the perceptive faculties of the physical body and all of its impressionistic channels are limited to the grossly mundane things of the physical world.

The eyes can only see to a limited extent and within a limited portion of the universal scale of vibrations. There are colors and tones too high and too low for the physical eyes to see. The physical ear cannot hear all of the sounds that exist in the universe, for its consciousness and its mechanical means of translation of impressions are limited to a certain low portion of the scale of vibrations. The same is true of tasting, smelling, and feeling. In other words, the human physical consciousness is a consciousness of itself and of its like throughout nature. It was created and placed in the cells of matter in order that matter might be conscious of itself in all physical forms; beyond that it has no consciousness and cannot perceive or comprehend.

Truly, man, in a physical sense, is a finite, mortal, limited creature, and without the breath of life, the soul, and the divine consciousness, is not "a living soul," but a mere aggregation of earthly substances with their limited form of earthly consciousness.

A violet growing in the green fields is an entity with a personality and character easily distinguished. Its characteristics of form, color, odor, cycle of birth and rebirth, and other distinguishing features constitute its personality. Its personality is the result of all of the consciousness within its body. A rose is distinguishable from all other flowers by its character or its personality. These are a result of the consciousness within it. Burbank learned that by modifying the consciousness of a flower or a piece of fruit through the introduction of a few cells of different consciousness, the outer and inner character and personality of flowers and fruit might be changed. Primitive man learned long ago that he could graft the personality of one tree into another by grafting some part of the physical consciousness or cell life of one into the other.

Returning to man again as our principal study, we find that the character and personality of man are the result of the thought consciousness within his being. And just as the character or personality of a flower, a tree, or a piece of mineral, or a piece of fruit is not exclusively manifested by the outer shape or form of the thing, so man's character and personality do not rest in the form of his body nor its size or weight, but in other subtle expressions of form, size, and color.

Realizing, then, that the consciousness within a man's body, like unto the consciousness within all things, is responsible for the distinct character or personality of man, we need think only of one other important point in order to have a perfect picture of man as a marvelous creation. That point is this: The soul consciousness added to the physical consciousness in the body of man during incarnation here on earth gives man his character or personality. Differing from those things which have no soul or divine consciousness, man's character or personality is not solely a result of the physical consciousness in his body, but the result of a blending or uniting, or cooperative action and reaction of the soul consciousness with, and upon, the physical consciousness. Thus, the dual consciousness of man constitutes his personality or character.

One final point in connection with this cosmic conception of the soul. As the physical consciousness in man changes through its physical evolution tending toward perfection, the physical characteristics of man change. As the soul consciousness in man is given more and more opportunity to express itself and to guide or dominate the thinking and the acting of man, so his character and personality will change. In other words, as the soul consciousness and the physical consciousness in man change through experience, through greater opportunities to express, through more complete understanding and comprehension, through more perfect attunement with the higher principles of life, so the character and personality of man change and evolve.

We now find that we have three reasons for the incarnation of the soul in the body. First, that—for a reason which we will explain shortly—the soul is to have certain earthly experiences; and, second, the human physical body is to have the advantage of spiritual knowledge and illumination in addition to its mundane knowledge; and third, that the character and personality of man may be perfected.

CHAPTER 6

THE PERSONALITY
OF THE SOUL

In the previous chapter we learned that one of the purposes of the soul's incarnation in the physical body is to assist in the building up of character and personality. This brings us to a consideration of what is character and what constitutes personality.

We have shown that all of the ancient and modern religions and philosophies conceded that the joining of the soul to the physical body results in "a living soul" on this earth. But we are not known as living souls but as certain characters and personalities, each distinctly different in many ways and classified only in certain broad generalities.

Our consideration, therefore, should be of what constitutes the personality of a living being. Character is generally considered as the ethical and moral principles which become the guide in life for each individual. Character, like individuality, is something that is not only constantly changing in many respects but is such a combination of elements of the physical self that it may be changed or modified at will. We mold our character, build our character, and establish our character by the things that we think, principles we hold fast to and adopt, and the acts we perform.

A banker as an individual is a banker only because that is his occupation or profession. The classification of a man as a banker refers more to his individuality and perhaps to his character than it does to his personality. The plumber likewise is classified as such because of his occupation or his trade. Some elements of character may enter into the determination of that classification, but his *personality* may be absolutely unknown even to those who have employed him the most often as a plumber. An actor is classified as such because of his profession but not likely because of his *character*. There may be traits or elements of nature in his character that would enable us to identify him as an actor or capable of playing the part of an actor, even though we know nothing of his *real personality*. The artist may have nothing about him which would identify him as an artist, but there may be traits in his character which reveal the artistic tendencies and abilities which he possesses. He may be occupied in his art and he may not be. Nevertheless, he may be classified as an artist although we lack knowledge of his personality.

Individuality and character may be so instantly altered as to mislead us in our judgment. We may know a certain person as a banker through our daily business transactions. He may be employed in a bank where we have met him for many years and the mere mention of his name brings to our minds the immediate classification of "banker." In his outer habits, manner of dress, and manner of business conversation he may reveal himself as a character properly classified as a "banker." But we may accidentally meet him some evening in his home and find him playing a violin or a piano so proficiently that we instantly discover that in character he is also a musician. His individuality, as far as clothes and mannerisms are concerned, may continue to show us that he is essentially a banker by profession, but we notice that he can cast aside this individuality or character of the daytime and become the musician in the evening. Still, we may know nothing of his *true personality.* We may meet him in the summertime in the grounds of his country home and find that he is also a very proficient and enthusiastic agriculturist. His long study of the subject of gardening, for instance, as a hobby may make him very expert in this classification and as we see him in his overalls with rake and hoe we see a different individual or character than the one of banker—and yet we may know nothing of *his personality.*

The dignified businessman who has held a responsible position and earned the popular faith in him as an efficient business executive may be tempted to commit some crime and we may find him later on in a penitentiary serving some period of time. Having been found in his crime and discovered in his false characterization of an honest, worthy, sincere businessman, he has now thrown off his cloak and reveals his individuality and character on a level with the other prisoners around him; and we may be surprised through his language and actions to learn that the mannerisms of speech and habit which he exhibited for so many years in his business office were merely superficial qualities worn as a cloak. We may now classify him not as a businessman but as a criminal. Still, we may know nothing whatever about his *real personality.*

I trust that I have enabled you to appreciate the difference between character and personality. Personality appears to be, therefore, that inner, private nature of our real selves which has little to do with all of our outer physical or mental characterizations. It is unquestionably true that the real personality of every individual will consciously and unconsciously affect the outer habits and mannerisms of the physical self. It is also true, however, that all of the outer characterizations do not constitute a perfect index to the real personality within.

The personality within us constitutes, in a mental phase, that which we actually believe, that which we actually know, and that which has become a positive conviction with us through our thinking and our experiences. In a spiritual sense the inner self is that which is closely associated with our deep emotions and with our silent, private, cosmic and spiritual experiences. In a moral sense our personality consists of those things which we have secretly and privately established as our immutable principles or code of life. In our actions our real personality influences us by the habits, customs, and mannerisms which we have adopted gradually and so profoundly that we are almost unaware of their existence and find it almost impossible to change them or modify them.

Briefly, we may say, therefore, that personality is the inner self, or the self that is being built up by the inner consciousness and the inner man. In contrast, character and individuality constitute the outer self, or that which is of the physical, mental consciousness.

A study of the human personality through psychology and psychiatry has revealed in the past several hundred years that it is gradually formed in each individual by external influences and internal influences. Some specialists in psychology call this inner personality the *subliminal self* or the *self-conscious self.* In a true classification, however, it should be called the *true personality.* It is undoubtedly true that through heredity we inherit some elements of our personality, and it is unquestionably true that we also acquire most of the elements of our personality through internal and external influences.

By internal influences I mean those urges, inspirations, ideas, and impulses that rise within our emotions as a result of spiritual or cosmic contact, or through the transmission of ideas and principles to the inner consciousness from the outer consciousness. Certain courses of study, certain pictures, selections of music, and experiences in life will establish ideas, principles, and convictions in the outer consciousness which, because of their agreeableness to our understanding or to our other elements of personality, are adopted by the personality as further points of modifications. Experiences in life which teach invaluable lessons and bring to our outer consciousness a conviction of the truth of some great law or principle which we accept as being universal in nature and helpful in our progress through life, are adopted by the inner personality as rules and laws unto itself.

Sorrow, pain, and suffering, and the sympathetic understanding of the sorrow and sufferings of others will soften some of the harsh elements in our own outer nature and carry some points of characterization into the inner personality and there become fixed as additional elements of the inner self. Meditation, prayer, spiritual visions, and similar experiences of the inner self constantly add elements to the evolving personality. In this way the personality of the self within is being gradually developed toward a degree of perfection which it did not have when it entered the physical body.

Because of the very intimate nature of the lessons learned by this inner self, and because of the confidential principles and ideals held by this inner self, the real personality of an individual being is known only to those most intimately associated with him and discovered only through long, intimate contact.

It has been found also, through a long study of the personality of man, that the tendency of the inner self is to build up a personality progressively toward a higher degree of perfection rather than toward a lower one. Regardless of how the *outer* man may live, and even pervert the morals and ethical principles to a continuously lower standard—as with the habitual criminal who is brazen and bold to the utmost degree—the *real personality within* is usually molding itself along lines that tend toward a higher standard and a greater degree of perfection.

It is a positive fact, revealed even by the action of confirmed criminals, that the higher ideals and more perfect standards of the inner self constantly challenge and question the actions of the outer self. Thus, most criminals sooner or later find themselves horribly annoyed and persecuted by a form of remorse actuated by what is sometimes called the *conscience,* but which is really the voice of the inner self or personality challenging the conduct of the outer self. Psychology in recent years has found a way to reach and arouse from its temporary imprisonment the inner personality of many persons to such an extent that a correct picture of the real self is revealed and the better tendencies of this inner self are given an opportunity to control the outer being.

The reason for the general upward tendency of the development of the inner personality is due, first of all, to the fact that it is closely associated with the Divine Consciousness in man and with those channels, or means of securing knowledge, which constantly inform the self of what is right, what is just, and what is merciful. Secondly, the outer self of man may deceive others through temporary modifications or coloring of its true nature, but the inner self of man cannot be deceived by the outer self nor can the outer self be deceived by the inner self. And, therefore, man in his own private periods of meditation and thoughtfulness knows what is right and what is wrong and is not deceived by any fictitious claim on the part of the physical consciousness. Thus, man tends toward higher thinking and self-improvement inwardly through his own private understanding of the real facts of life, while outwardly he may not be conforming to the standards thus being established.

—

CHAPTER 7

DOES PERSONALITY SURVIVE TRANSITION?

In any analysis of this question we are confronted by two distinct and opposed claims. One is a theological doctrine; the other is called a scientific conclusion. Both of them are accepted by a large number of persons on faith. Both of them are sustained by the same kind of evidence when presented by the average representative of the school supporting them.

To proceed properly, let us place in a few words the two opposing claims in regard to man's destiny:

1. The theory of theology that man possesses an immortal *soul* or *personality* which survives the death of his body.

2. The theory of materialistic science that man's *individualism* or *personality* begins at the birth of his body and ends with the death of his body.

Let us note that the words used in these two brief contentions are carefully chosen. In number two the word *soul* is not used. Materialism does not recognize the existence of a soul, but does admit the very positive existence of that "something" labeled *personality* or *individuality*. The term *materialistic science* is used to distinguish one form of "science" from the many. Likewise, in number one the words *soul* and *personality* are joined as synonymous only because theology *assumes* such to be representative of a fact.

The question of man's destiny, or the fate of his "personality" after the death of the body, is so old that its origin is lost in antiquity. The earliest records of man's thinking indicate that the discussion was a common and familiar one with but three conclusions as possible answers. In fact, we find that the materialistic conclusion was held by the minority of ancient civilization as today; and the majority sincerely held to the other. In all ages this conclusion or doctrine was philosophical, and not purely theological, as man has tried to make it in recent centuries.

We should not be considered presumptuous when we compare these various conclusions and beliefs, if it is our desire to find which of them is most in harmony with justice and which does the least violence to our natural feelings.

The materialistic doctrine is born of and based upon the *assumption* that man is born a helpless, ignorant infant as a product of an unknown principle called *heredity*, operating through or with forces and impulses of which he knows nothing and cannot combat; that, therefore, he possesses as advantages and handicaps, certain abilities, tendencies, fortitudes, and weaknesses, for the possession of which *he is in no way responsible.* Why he was born at all, why he is *what* he is, and to what end, he does not know and cannot know.

He tries to reconcile conditions, as he finds them, with the doctrine of materialistic heredity—regardless of the many manifest contradictions; for his doctrine says that the thief, the murderer, the fool, the liar, and the depraved have but inherited the endowment of their forebears; while the good, the noble, the rich, the happy, and the prosperous have unconsciously, mechanically, or *simply,* received the blessings passed by preceding generations. Such a doctrine does not account for the birth of a thief or a murderer in a long line of honorable ancestors, nor the birth of a noble, fortunate one in a family tree "rotten to the roots."

The believers of such a doctrine contend that they should not be condemned for their frailties, tendencies, or commissions. Even man-made laws excuse conditions thrust upon one by another without contributory responsibility or warrant, and even the most savage races would not tolerate— let alone create—a law which justified the punishment of one man for the sins—or commissions—of another.

Such beliefs as this preclude the possibility of a Divine Intelligence concerned in the birth and existence of man, individually and even collectively, and eliminate the existence of divine consciousness or soul in man of a nature distinct from the material essence of chemical life in his body.

Therefore, says material science, man is a chemical product—the result of mechanical or systematic laws which automatically carry on their processes of reproduction without conscious intelligence. Man is just born as he is, what he is, struggles to modify the blind, indifferent laws of nature, and eventually succumbs to the inevitable breaking-down processes of the material elements—and dies. That is the end of man—again, individually and collectively.

A doctrine of *fatalism* is the religious creed of the materialistic believers. That we are born men—a certain type of chemical product—instead of monkeys, rats, or cattle, is due to chance. Our place in the animal kingdom is due to lottery. We have come from nowhere—by no real law that would prove itself by and through justice, mercy, forgiveness, consideration, or love—and pass on to nowhere again.

The good men and the just in the world are deserving of no more credit for their qualities than are the evil deserving of condemnation or punishment. Just as our tendencies, abilities, weaknesses, and prowesses are inherited without our sanction—or conscious warrant—so our experiences, fortunes, sorrows, joys, successes, and failures throughout life are acquired by us without deserving them and without moral or personal responsibility.

If we can cheat the system by beating the game of life in any move, if we can frustrate blind principles by our own developed sight, or build where tearing down seems imminent, we prove our individual strength and fitness to survive the decree of fate. The belief in eternal justice, law, order, goodness, and love is but a delusion. The law of right overpowering might, and character determining destiny is but a childish illusion—so declares the doctrine of materialism!

The theological doctrine—like unto the materialistic one—includes an assumption, viz: that the soul or personality of each individual being is *uniquely created* for each existence by God through immutable laws and principles known only to God. While this doctrine *seems* to be a great and inspiring relief from the depressing viewpoint of the materialist—and for that reason has become the hope of many—it is found, upon analysis and experience, unsatisfying to progressive, thinking minds.

We discover, first, that although it transfers the authorship of our creation from blind, unconscious chemical action to God, man remains a creature made and born from the nowhere, and the credit or responsibility for his existence rests with a personal maker and not with the process. Man is still a creature of circumstance and free from the responsibility of his creation, his existence, or his equipment, mentally, spiritually, or physically.

By attributing to the personalized creative power—God—that which we could not attribute to the impersonal creative, chemical processes, we have our *responsibility* for our existence endowed with conscious understanding, omnipotent power, infinite wisdom, and universal purpose.

The very first of these endowments—conscious understanding—warrants our belief in universal law, order, system, and purpose. To create knowingly, to cause consciously and permit understandingly, God must have a purpose, a plan, a scheme of things. There can be no element of chance, no lottery, no accident. All must be by decree. Hence man is, again, and after all, a creature of fate—divine, spiritual, infinite though it may be.

Likewise, if man is the creature of such a Creator, he, the creature, must be in possession of some of the attributes of his Creator; he must have the wisdom, power, and understanding, to some degree, of the essence from which he emanated. He must inherit—through his ancestral heredity—that infinite equipment which theology calls *soul* and which it intimates is synonymous with "personality."

Theology proceeds a step further in its explanation of man's inherited possessions and states dogmatically or logically—however you may view the point—that since the consciousness, wisdom, and power of God and man are of a universal and eternal nature, the soul of man is therefore eternal, *immortal.*

As we have said, the theological doctrine is different from the materialistic one in only a few elements. It still leaves man the creature of fate. It relieves him of all responsibility for his birth, his existence, his endowments, and his heritage. A theological problem is involved in such a doctrine and requires explanation; and theology meets the issue quite conveniently.

The creator of man, possessing understanding, omnipotent power, and infinite wisdom, working through a universal purpose, must wilfully permit, at least, the sufferings, sins, and errors of his offspring. Hence, God must either be indifferent toward his creatures or positively approving of these things. And, since there is a universal purpose in God's consciousness, he must approve of man's sufferings as well as man's joys.

At once we find ourselves face to face with involved theological doctrines, creeds, and dogmas which include *predestination* and revenge.

Predestination, as set forth in the Westminster Confession of Faith, is the doctrine which reveals that: "By the decree of God, for the manifestation of His Glory, some men and angels are predestined into everlasting life and others foreordained to everlasting death . . . whereby He extendeth or withholdeth mercy, as He pleaseth, for the Glory of His Sovereign Power over His creatures."

The principle of revenge or retribution is set forth in the Second Commandment (Exodus 20:5): "For I the Lord Thy God am a jealous God, visiting the iniquity of the fathers upon the children unto the third and fourth generation of them that hate me; . . ."

Practically all of the theological controversies of the past have arisen through attempts to reconcile the theological principle of *fatalism* with *infinite* or even *mundane justice.* One of the results has been a tendency to shift the responsibility for the evil in men's lives to a satanic character. Even this leaves open the contentions regarding predestination, free will, the original sin of Adam and the atonement for it.

For, according to the theological principles quoted above, man is created arbitrarily and without his desire, and at the moment of creation is either *blessed* or *damned* eternally. Hence, man is either good or evil, fortunate or unfortunate, noble or depraved, from the first step in the process of his physical creation to the moment of his last breath, regardless of his individual desires, hopes, ambitions, struggles, or devoted prayers.

Such is theological fatalism! Does it offer any consolation when compared to the principle of material fatalism? Only our deeper and truly mystical conception of God's real laws and purposes enables us to see behind these theological creeds and dogmas and find the truth.

Is it any wonder that progressive, searching, sincere men and women in all lands object to the narrowness of the theological creeds which permit such conclusions to be reached as we have in the foregoing paragraphs?

The principle of justice in all things—especially in the course of life—demands that man shall earn what he gets, deserve what he requires, and merit what he seeks; likewise, it assures man that he shall not get what he has not earned or deserved. The law of *reaping what we sow* is not a theological, religious, or ethical decree, but a scientific, philosophical, and moral principle, the basis of justice.

The idea that man must suffer the sins of another, solely because the other was sinful through the fatalistic decree of his Maker at the time of his making, is certainly contrary to the principles of *human justice,* let alone *divine justice.* That one creature is good because the Maker planted good in him and another is bad because the Maker planted evil in him— forever and eternally, unalterably and irremediably—is most surely unfair to all mankind. But that the evil men should have their unearned or undeserved sins transmitted to their offspring "unto the third and fourth generation" is the utmost of *injustice.*

Thus the doctrine that all men are sinners and have the essential sin of Adam is a challenge to justice, mercy, love, and omnipotent fairness. Of course, if it is necessary to *assume* that *fatalistic man* can sin against the omnipotent and infinite will or decree of his Maker, then the sin of Adam was strictly his own by permission or tolerance of God, and he alone could compensate for his sin. On the other hand, if mankind—forever and forever—sinned through Adam, then man alone should compensate through personal, individual suffering. Therefore, the doctrine of atonement, whereby man's responsibility for his essential sin was shifted to another to be paid by crucifixion, is also opposed to justice.

Salvation through right living is impossible, according to these doctrines, for man cannot be saved through personal merit, since he has none—for all that is good in him, of him, and through him belongs to his Maker who decreed and fore-ordained it.

Man so loves *justice*, and has through the ages developed a so much better and more noble idea of justice—regardless of its seeming absence in the *theological scheme* of things—that he has refused to countenance, let alone support or encourage, the doctrines of either materialistic or theological fatalism. No successful scheme of conduct in life, either moral or ethical, least of all religious, can be built upon the theory that we are, from the primary phase of our creation, and for no merit or demerit of our own, either the favorites of God's arbitrary blessings or the blind victims of his vengeance and wrath.

Therefore man seeks the truth—and his essential desire is to see justice done to the wisdom and power of God as well as to the interests of God's creatures. This is what the true modernist seeks; it is what the mystic of all ages has demanded.

CHAPTER 8

HEREDITY AND INHERITANCE

The body of a child is not *created* but reorganized from preexisting elements. Every element entering into its physical make-up has always existed since "the beginning" and will always exist—even after the "death" of the body. Chemically these elements are either pure or impure, according to the nature of the environment in which they are assembled or the contamination by impure "seeds sown to be reaped."

Heredity is the process of modifying the pure stream and straight line of ascent of the body's physical evolution. It relates exclusively to the material elements of the body as transmitted or contributed by the preceding period of evolution, the preceding generation of existence.

A period of reincarnation for the *physical body* begins at the moment when preexisting elements are drawn together to re-form an organized body, and ends when the magnetic influence—life—ceases to hold the elements together; and these elements separate and return "unto the dust of the earth" again. From conception, or unification, unto "death" is one half the cycle of *physical evolution* of each body. From dissolution or "death" unto unification again is the other half of the cycle.

The second half of the cycle is as essential to the process of evolution as the first half. Through dissolution or de-composition of the elements of the body they are freed from any abnormal or unnatural associations they may have been forced into by man's wilful violation of nature's laws. Dis-ease is the result of abnormal, subnormal, or inharmonious relation or association of elements in a part or parts of the body. Perfect health is pure harmonium of elemental rela-tionship.

"Death"—or dissolution—is nature's economical method of ending the stress and struggle between the inharmonious elements for dominion and power, and the first step in the process of the return to a pure, normal, natural state and environment of each element. Thus, dissolution is the phase of physical evolution which is cleansing, purging, and reha-bilitating.

From the rehabilitation state each element is attracted again by the magnetic influence of reconstructing life, and finds its way to association, organization, and group mani-festation.

In the procedure from rehabilitated primary state to recomposition in a new group form, these elements may become contaminated, or have forced into their general as-sembly some disadvantageous or impure elements. In this manner the very first and later stages of physical evolution, *prior to birth,* may prove to be qualifying stages of nor-malcy. This, and this alone, is *heredity*—what the larger, parent body has sown. The offspring will harvest what its parent has planted. The lesser part experiences the effects of the acts of the larger part, while the larger bears the responsibility and must compensate. It is the law of justice in magnificent demonstration.

When the soul enters the physical body it takes residence within a physical form prepared, in purity or contamination, to receive it. The physical form has no choice in the selection of the soul to be its companion through the forthcoming cycle of existence. The soul, on the other hand, has no free choice in the selection of the body in which it is to be imprisoned or glorified for another period of incarnation. Both are drawn together, attracted to each other, and united by the law of compensation—the law of justice.

The soul comes forth from its eternal abode with its consciousness and personality unimpaired by the changes in the mortal body from which it was freed at "death" or transition. It is not composed of dissimilar elements or temporary associates. It is one entity, uncomposed, uncreated, and undivided. It is the very antithesis of the physical body in every characteristic. Whatever may distinguish the physical body is a negative expression of the soul's positive character.

The soul possesses, as a heritage from the Infinite Consciousness and Mind "in the beginning," a *mind and memory,* constituting a continuity of experience which is eternal. It is this consciousness of self, this *mind and memory*, which we characterize as *personality*, then, which grows and is molded into greater comprehension and power through the various cycles of evolution.

Into the physical body comes the soul with its personality, its perfect memory of all past experiences and its acquired penalties and rewards earned through the Law of

Compensation. It is still free to choose, free to decide, free to submit or to rebuke the urges which comes from its memory of past experiences or the whisperings of the world without. But it has debits and credits to its record from the past and these it cannot avoid.

Whatever it may decide to do, it must contend with the Law of Compensation in attempting to carry out its decisions. The debt to be paid will be demanded by the Law of Karma at the moment which is most propitious. Ever and anon the silent adjuster of the law stands by and with the nod of his head permits the decision of man to come to an issue or to fail.

Karma is not revengeful. It would be self-annihilating if revenge or retribution were its motives. It can only be re-creative and constructive. The progressive evolution and advancement of the personality is its sole purpose.

It demands not "an eye for and eye and a tooth for a tooth," as does the law which man invented as his imitation of the Law of Compensation. It demands only justice—justice to *all*, the sinner and the one sinned against, the benefactor and the one benefited. It has the power to carry out its principles. It leaves nothing to the judgment of man, for he had his choice and decided; it retains the sole responsibility for its operation, for man agreed to this when he decided. Its aim is guidance; its methods are instructive; its functions are redeeming. Such is the Law of Karma.

Karma selects for its *propitious time* to exact compensation or bestow blessings that moment in the period of the soul's residence within the physical body when the personality will profit most by the lesson to be learned, the experience to be realized, or the reward to be utilized to the betterment of all concerned.

It selects for its place of manifestation that localization of events which is most favorable for an impressive demonstration to all who may discern and profit thereby. It selects for its means of action or medium of performance those channels which will afford the utmost of efficiency and direction in compensative adjustment, with consideration for every living creature.

Since Karma seeks neither revenge nor retribution, but exacts only an adequate adjustment of conditions, a balancing of realization—that man may become more perfect in conduct—it may elect to suspend an objective compensation in favor of a subjective penitence.

If the personality of man is brought face to face with a situation in life which clearly reveals itself as a karmic debt to be cancelled by a trying experience, it may find the experience modified, the test lightened, or the suffering eased, by *acknowledging the justice of the debt,* and discovering the lesson contained therein. With appreciation for the knowledge, and with penitent heart for the error previously committed, the personality may find that the ends of justice and Karma have been satisfied. Thus the principles of salvation by grace, and redemption by atonement, have their real origin in the just working of a great law.

We discover in reincarnation and Karma the only rational and acceptable explanation and cause for the seeming injustice of the inequalities of life.

Some are born in wealth, some in abject poverty; some are born with every advantage for education and advancement, some with no opportunity at all. One is born handicapped, physically and mentally; another is born without flaw. In a given family of four children, one is strong and healthy of body but mentally defective; another is born sickly and with a weak body, but brilliant in mind; one is born with cruel, mean, sordid tendencies, bringing shame to all the others; and the fourth is serious and noble, with religious ideals.

Heredity alone cannot account for all the physical defects endowed at birth; it cannot always account for the physical differences in the various children in one family. Nor can materialistic or theological fatalism explain—with satisfaction and justice—the inequalities found in each race, each nation, or even each group of men.

The Law of Reincarnation alone makes understandable and acceptable the conditions and experiences of our lives.

I am tomorrow, or some future day, what I establish today. I am today what I established yesterday—or some previous day.

I may be as unmindful of things I do to establish my Karma as I am unmindful of many of the results of Karma.

I may be enjoying good health in this incarnation without appreciating the fact that I earned it, deserved it, or established it, by some acts or attitude of mine in the past. And I may show so little appreciation for this blessing of health, and so neglect its possession, that some day I shall suffer poor health—either in this incarnation or another.

I may possess those desirable endowments which others do not have, and simply take them for granted. I may elaborate upon the things I do not possess and consider my lot peculiar, accursed, and damned.

Each of us from our personal point of view is prone to measure the inequalities of life by the yardstick of his needs, and to overlook his blessings. If, however, we consider the good things we possess as natural birthrights, deserved or earned in some way, we should be consistent enough to look upon our afflictions as similarly deserved or earned. As soon as man looks upon his whole station in life as his birthright, rather than just the half that is acceptable, he will be ready to meet his Karma and work it out.

How careful man is to guard his fortunes lest he lose them by some act that would justify the loss! How concerned he is that he may commit some act or fail to do something that will automatically, logically, and fairly turn the blessings of his life into other channels. Yet he fails to realize that the afflictions, adversities, weaknesses, and crosses in his life may be transformed, transmuted, and transcended in the same manner.

Thus we see that the inequalities in life are karmic and, in accordance with the Law of Karma, are adjustable. Thus man's fate is *ever in the molding,* and man alone bears the *responsibility.*

The full course of man's life is *not* one incarnation on earth in one physical body. To assume or believe it is, is to say that the elements of the physical body—matter—never cease to exist, never *die,* or become annihilated, but man's personality and soul come into existence, manifest for a time, and then cease to function.

We see, plainly, that the existence of matter is one continuous cycle of periodic re-formations, of expressions, never ceasing to manifest, retaining its essential nature always, but reborn in a new form in accordance with the immutable laws of the universe.

The *personality* of man has its course of existence, eternal and continuous. Each personality came into existence "in the beginning of all creation," and has always existed and will exist into eternity.

The course of such existence for each personality is marked by definite periods of rebirth in a physical body—a new medium of expression. We call each period of existence in the body an *incarnation,* for the personality or soul is incarnated in the flesh. The successive incarnations are reincarnations or rebirths in physical bodies.

From birth to birth, or rebirth to rebirth, is a *period of evolution* for the soul or personality. This period may be divided into two phases: (a) the *mundane phase*—from rebirth to transition; and (b) the *cosmic phase*—from transition to rebirth. We may consider the entire line of the course of existence of the personality as eternally moving forward in undulating phases.

The very terminology used in this schematic illustration is suggestive of laws and principles. It is borrowed from the teachings of the Rosicrucians, the most highly evolved group of mystics living in all ages, whose knowledge of God's laws and nature's ways is most profound.

CHAPTER 9

KARMA AND PERSONAL EVOLUTION

M an is not discouraged or disheartened in his quest for perfection by learning from experience that there are certain immutable laws universally established. Nor is he checked, in his determination to attain the heights of his ambition, by discovering that these immutable laws are *impersonal* and *impartial*. That these laws affect all of God's children, and even every species of living things, regardless of parental heritage, social standing, financial power, or divine attunements, makes man see in and through them a principle of real justice.

The mystic claims that it is the continued demonstration of the immutable laws of nature which proves the existence of an Infinite Mind and Omnipotent Power, inspired by Love, Mercy, and Justice.

Unquestionably it is the evidence of the workings of these immutable laws that has maintained and sustained the faith of millions of people, in all ages, in the existence of some fair, just, and Infinite Intelligence ruling the universe. It has been this faith—aye, even conviction—that has saved the world from self-damnation and self-destruction; and it is this same conviction, growing more and more convincing through test and demonstration in science and every phase of common experience, that is responsible for the worldwide challenge of the truth of certain theological doctrines.

Man is truly becoming more and more religious in his thinking and living, and less theological. This is detrimental to some of the churches, but joyous for the Kingdom of God.

What are the fundamental *immutable* laws? First, that matter and energy are indestructible. Fire, decay, the will of man, the decree of God, may change, modify, or redirect the manifestation and nature of matter, but nothing can destroy its essential existence. Energy—the fundamental, universal essence of all power—may be directed and redirected in its course of action and demonstration, but it cannot be destroyed any more than it can be created. It has always existed and always will exist.

Man has come to understand the principle of immutability so well that he realizes that even the Master who originally conceived and decreed these immutable laws and set them into action with the "Word" (Logos) cannot now suspend, modify, or abrogate them. One incident of suspension, one demonstration of modification, would rob those laws of their universal justice. But neither history nor tradition record a single authentic instance where even the least important laws of nature has been changed.

What a marvelous conception in the beginning! What wonderful system, order, and law of equity! How our hopes rise and our fears fade away in the knowledge of sublime justice for all—every created and living thing. Truly, God was just and fair—in the beginning! Why should we doubt that God is *still* just?

Another immutable law is that we shall reap as we sow; the tendency on the part of every living cell to reproduce its own nature plus some degree of progression in its evolution. Against varying odds, wilful interference on the part of man, and the influence of environment and unrelated forces of nature, the tendency of every living thing is to be true to type, even reverting to type when forced for a while to accept unwarranted modifications. As a companion principle, we have what is generally known as the Law of Compensation, or "Karma," as the mystics of many ages have called it.

The work of Luther Burbank was possible only because of nature's immutable laws. By continually blending the elements of nature in accordance with the laws of synthesis, man has reaped a harvest of testimonies to the law. "If but once man in any part of the world should reap an orange from planted watermelon seeds, our faith in the whole scheme of living would be shattered!" said an eminent clergyman in England some years ago. If man should ever discover a single instance when the Law of Compensation or automatic adjustment did not operate in nature's normal processes, he would be justified in losing all faith in the infinite wisdom of the Universal Mind.

An ancient philosopher, who was truly a mystic, expressed the greatest principle of creation by saying that all things "are becoming." Each hour of the day every material thing is becoming something else. It is the law of change, of motion, of life.

In the whole universe there is nothing today that is *new* in existence. Nothing has been *created* since the beginning when the "Word" established all *created things;* and, as we have said, nothing has been destroyed or ever will be destroyed.

All is unceasing, *progressive* change. This is the true law of evolution. The mystic knows that man as a species has been and is *evolving*—not from a lower species, but from a lesser to a greater degree of perfection. In the beginning was the Word and the Word was made flesh; and man as a species was conceived and created simultaneously with all living creatures resembling him in some characteristics. But primitive man was as far advanced beyond the ape as modern man is advanced beyond the primitive progenitors of his type. He has evolved more rapidly than all other species of the animal kingdom because of endowments not possessed by other creatures.

All that which seems like "creating" is "re-creating"— evolution, change. All that which seems destructive is but a phase in the process of constructive change. It is also evolution. Therefore, all that which is loosely called *creation* and *annihilation* is really transformation. That which seems new is but old matter, old thought, old spirit, old life, old hate, old evil, old errors, in new forms, new births of manifestation. There are no contradictions in nature's laws. Harmony is the element that binds them all into one law—the Law of Evolution.

Since there is no destruction of matter, energy, force, or principle, and no creation of this from what has not always existed "from the beginning," all is eternal, immortal. Hence, even the body of man in its elements, the spirit of life in its essence, the soul of man in its consciousness, are eternal and immortal.

There must be a law of evolution—change—new form for the mind, character, personality, and soul of man, as there is for the physical body of man. Coincident with the gradual, progressive evolution of man's physical body in the ages of the past has been the progressive evolution of the soul of man.

The soul in man—or call it mind, personality, or character—is the flower of God's creation, the acme of nature's products. It is inconceivable that nature should give immortality, and the accompanying opportunity to evolve, to the least speck of unconscious dust and deny it to the soul of man.

We have intimated that the soul in man is associated with personality, and that it has a conscious *mind.*

There is hardly any basis for argument in the statement that man is a dual being. Without the least consideration of any of the ancient or modern philosophies we can say in simple words that man, as a sentient entity, is a physical being through which expresses a *personality,* individuality, or distinct character. Essentially, man is partly physical and partly non-physical; partly material and partly immaterial.

In this duality we sense a unity of different beings. That we are warranted in looking upon the personality or soul of man as a *spiritual being* within the physical body is indicated by the many common experiences of life quite independent of the principles expounded by psychology.

The experiences commonly designated as *dreams* reveal at least that man may be conscious of his existence and conscious of the world, without any functioning on the part of his waking consciousness. Whatever way we analyze dreams and conclude that they are the result of restlessness on the part of the brain or mind, the fact remains that the consciousness of the self during dreams is not the same as the self-consciousness during our normal waking conditions, in either degree or nature.

On the other hand, there are those occasions when this consciousness of self is asleep or dormant while the physical body is active and more than normally functioning; as, for instance, when chloroform or ether is used to dull the consciousness while the body is kept active through handling, abuse, and trial.

There is that very large class of frequent phenomena typified by the experience in which the consciousness of one in profound meditation seems to leave the physical body and, as a sentient being, goes out into space and revels in environments far removed from the locality of the physical body. At such times there is always a distinct sense of the separateness of the material and immaterial selves.

What is this inner self? Theology answers and says, "the soul." Philosophy answers and says it is "consciousness of self." The mystic—ever more guarded and precise than the theologian or the philosopher—says, "It is the personality or ego!"

Personality or ego is the consciousness of the spiritual body—the soul. It is the part of dual man that has been progressively evolving along with the evolution of the physical body. Just as the physical body has gradually acquired a more upright position, a more tranquil expression, and a more refined form, so the personality—or consciousness of the soul—has evolved a more universal knowledge, a more intimate acquaintance with itself, and a more idealistic relation of its purpose in life. This development of the consciousness of personality in man is conveniently called *personal evolution.* The purpose of such evolution is to build character.

Every ethical and moral system of the past and present has had for its aim the building or perfecting of character. Even the primary stages of elementary education contribute greatly—for good or bad—in the molding of character. The Greeks adopted a system, now being revived, of character molding *before birth*, through the prenatal influences of the mother. Unquestionably education has the most formidable influence upon character, while religion, ethics, and morals—as codes and creeds—contribute a refining element.

It is the desire of every progressive, thinking being to develop the character to a degree of nobility and perfection where it is not only a personal asset—assuring very definite dividends—but an asset to the family, the city, and the nation.

We are told that *character is salvation.* Through the development of character man discovers himself and rounds out his dormant abilities while rounding off the rough corners of his nature. Truly, in this sense, the evolution of character is the approach to salvation from failure, sin, and ignominy.

Character is fate! Certainly, as we build our character in the *now,* we decree our fate in the future. The forcefulness of the truth of this statement needs no amplification.

Every experience in life, every incident consciously realized—and many of which we are unconscious, form a part of our molding personality. We are not only *now* what we *think*, but we will become that which results from our thinking. We are reaping daily and hourly as we have sown. Each day we become, mentally, spiritually, and physically what we have made ourselves. Hence, we are forever working out our own salvation or damnation, independent of the subtle influences of heredity, and independent of any predestined course in life.

Man possesses the power to choose. Free will is a fundamental factor of his highly developed—evolved—consciousness. But as he chooses, so must he abide. The responsibility rests with *him*. As he sows, so must he reap; as he obligates, so must he compensate; as he demands, so must he pay.

Man's life is an endless battle between urge and decision. Cosmic, divine inspirations from the consciousness *within* vie with worldly, material, gross temptations from without. Man is motivated by urge; he is free to decide and he *becomes* what he thereby decrees. Such is the principle, the true law of fatalism. The responsibility rests not in some blind law of chemical action and reaction, nor with a jealous, revengeful God.

Man may be blind to the consequences of his decisions, and may often be blind to the true nature of the urge which brings the need for decision. But the *immutable laws* provide one direct benefit as a result of every decision, every act. As man chooses—sows—so shall he reap and pay. That is the Law of Compensation.

According to this law, nature in every department of manifestation demands justice, equalization, and compensation. It is so old in the understanding of man that most of his self-made laws, even among primitive tribes and races, are based upon observations of its working.

The manifestation of the Law of Compensation constitutes the *great school of experience.* Through this school man has come to learn of his powers and limitations, his weaknesses and strengths, his advantage over all other living creatures. From childhood until old age, man learns that his evil acts are essentially a sin against his own career for which he must suffer or pay. He learns, too, that his noble deeds, unselfish acts, and idealistic thoughts bring their balanced rewards.

Each experience with the Law of Compensation adds to the molding of his creed in life, his guide of conduct, his code of thinking. The memory of each experience—each lesson—remains as a stone in the structure of the character that he is building. Personality—or character—is thereby evolving from childhood onward through every hour of conscious existence.

Thus the soul in man, the immaterial part of his dual being, the consciousness of the self, is an evolving entity which the mystics call *personality* or *ego*. And because of its very nature, because of its association with the immaterial part of his being, *personality is a spiritual, eternal, immortal entity.*

The following statements are not presented as the component elements of a mere doctrine, but as the essential parts or related phases of a law.

That reincarnation, as a doctrine, affords a more satisfactory explanation of life and its trials, tribulations, and compensations is apparent from the fact that it does not require a basic assumption other than that already adopted by all Christian and nearly all other forms of religious beliefs—the immortality of the soul.

On the other hand, it does not require the acceptance, upon faith, of any principle of fatalism, predestination, or retribution, operating through blind, material action or a revengeful, jealous God. Neither does it shift the responsibility of our fate from earthly atom to heavenly deity, but leaves it resting surely upon the individual.

Let us see, therefore, what the fundamental *assumption,* referred to above, means.

The soul, with its consciousness or personality, is *immortal.* This is the assumption and contention of all Christian doctrines and practically all other religions. The mystic claims that if the soul of man is something which is created anew and given existence for the first time when it enters a physical body, then it would cease to exist at that change of dual existence called *death* or *transition*—for if the soul of man is immortal *after death,* it must have been immortal *before birth.*

The immutable laws of nature prove to us that it is inconsistent with the whole scheme of nature to suppose, assume, or believe that the soul which enters each new body is an eternal, immortal entity created for the first time for each body, but living eternally thereafter.

The idea that the soul is immortal *only after it leaves the physical body* is but half of the truth, if true at all. That which is immortal *is* and *was* forever immortal. Immortality is not an element or quality that can be called into sudden existence and added to a thing to serve for an indefinite period of time. If it *is* at all, it must have been eternally.

Furthermore, if the soul in man is a gift, or an endowment from the Cosmic or the Infinite Consciousness or God, it must be of the essence or nature of the Infinite God—eternally immortal. It must have existed "in the beginning" and will exist into eternity. There can be no periodic creation of *new* parts or segments of the Divine Consciousness. Such a thought is so inconsistent with all other laws of nature that its belief is abhorrent to the real thinker.

Our only conclusion must be that the soul of man, with its consciousness of self, or personality, is preexistent, immortal, and eternal. It has always existed, but passes through the universal process of change.

The physical body of man, as we have seen, has attained its present degree of high perfection in appearance, form, nature, and functioning through progressive cycles of evolution. In all direct family lines of ascent we find that each generation of the blood, each cycle of the physical rebirth of the body, shows the effect of physical evolution, *if no evil seeds have been sown to be reaped.*

And coincident with these cycles of evolution—periods of rebirth along one line of ascent—the soul also evolves in cycles of existence along one line of ascent. Likewise the soul of man in each existence, in each reincarnation in a physical body, shows the effect of mental and spiritual evolution, *if no evil seeds have been sown to be reaped.*

CHAPTER 10

THE AGGREGATION
OF PERSONALITIES

It would appear from what has been said in the foregoing pages that since man evolves a distinctly different or modified personality in each earthly incarnation, these personalities, being an attribute of the soul, would give to each individual on earth an aggregation of the personalities previously evolved.

In other words, if the soul upon entrance into the physical body at birth carries with it any remnant of the personality or personalities possessed by it through previous incarnations, each one of us would possess at the present time in the present incarnation an aggregation of personalities rather than a single one.

The truth of the matter is that each one of us manifests primarily in each incarnation only *one* personality, and that one is that which is being evolved at the time; but this evolving personality is unquestionably an aggregation of the essential elements of the previous personalities possessed by the soul. Herein lies the only logical explanation for the commonplace manifestation of those complexes which psychoanalysis and psychiatry attempt to distinguish and separate into distinct traits or elements of character.

Merely as a hypothetical example, let us assume that we have before us for critical study a businessman, forty-five years of age, who has risen to his position from a family living in moderate circumstances and of average intellect. Let us assume that his schooling was derived exclusively in the public schools, with no college or special academic training, and that after entering the business world and contacting various occupations he finally entered the employ of a firm wherein diligent application, some special abilities, loyalty, and sincerity enabled him to become promoted until at the age of forty-five he reached the position of general manager, and is now a married man with two children, a fine home, a good income, a well-trained mind, with the advantages of some travel and much reading, and the benefits of culture and good social position to make the remainder of his life one of assured happiness and peace.

And let us assume, in our study of him, that while he is not an extremist in religious thought he is a supporter of the church and of every humanitarian, religious activity, is fond of wholesome outdoor sports, is conservative and dignified in his personal habits and language, steady and logical in his thinking, reasoning, and general activities, and given to one or two hobbies for relaxation. In general, he is neither a special study for the psychoanalyst nor one to be cast aside as having no complexes of any kind. In other words, he is just the average successful businessman whose personality and character seem to have been softened by many experiences and whose life is not affected by any of the passing thrills or momentary excitements of the day; yet he has shown unique ability in a number of directions and holds a number of convictions in his mind which nothing can reverse or modify. To his intimate friends he has a personality that is distinct enough to be recognized and distinguished from others, yet there are a few elements of this personality which appear to be foreign to it or at least unexpected variations.

From the viewpoint of those who do not believe in reincarnation this man's character and personality would be the result of his education, training, and experiences in the past forty-five years of this one incarnation exclusively. In other words, his present personality would be solely that which has evolved during this one incarnation.

From another point of view this personality is a blending and an aggregation of the essential and outstanding elements of his character and personality in all of his previous incarnations. In other words, we will assume that this man in his last incarnation was essentially a soldier, for most of his life was devoted to army training and to military experiences plus a few lessons of life learned through separation from his family, through a lack of sufficient income to give him in the latter part of his life the luxuries that he would have enjoyed, and similar experiences.

And we will assume that in the incarnation preceding that of a soldier he was essentially a physician, or one devoted to the study of disease and the practice of any methods that would relieve diseases and physical suffering, and that through this training and experience he learned many serious lessons of life, which, before the close of his incarnation, left indelible convictions upon his memory as elements of his personality.

And we will assume that in the incarnation preceding that of the physician he was a farmer in a provincial sense in some country bordering the Mediterranean, and that, as such, he learned through experience many other lessons of life, especially those relating to agriculture, the conservation of small funds, the benefits of diligent effort and watchfulness, the value of sacrifice, and the benefits of saving, as well as the detriments of the lack of education and the lack of opportunity to improve the mind and hand in practical application.

Without going back any farther in possible incarnations preceding these, we will see now that upon each transition this man carried in his soul and personality certain keenly learned lessons, or extremely well-learned experiences, which constitute at the present time the foundation stones or principal elements of his character and personality. If we look upon these outstanding lessons of each incarnation as rules and guides of life, written down in a ledger as the immutable laws by which he would govern himself, we will find that as he passed through each incarnation and added to the character ledger of his life, he also added new rules, new laws, new convictions, new elements of personality.

When he passed from the life of a farmer, and through reincarnation became the physician, he entered into a new life with some of the outstanding lessons he had learned as a farmer written secretly but indelibly in the inner nature of his being; and as he passed through childhood and studied to become a physician these deeply buried elements of his previous personality subtly manifested themselves by acting as controls or guides, or modifying tendencies, in the situations which confronted him in his daily life. Perhaps as a physician he may often have wondered at his inner liking for agriculture. Perhaps he wondered, also, about his deep-seated tendency to be saving, economical, and conservative in his expenditures. Undoubtedly he would have no recollection of having acquired these principles through experiences in a previous life. As he learned more lessons through his profession as a physician, new rules were established and new elements of personality were adopted and the rough and uncouth elements of his life as a farmer were eliminated, and at the close of his incarnation as a physician his personality was that of a blending of the principal elements of both the farmer and the physician.

When he came into life again in another incarnation as the soldier, he probably found early in his youth that he had a liking for the study of the human body and desired to know more about the organs and functionings of parts of the body, while at the same time upon occasion there may have been an uprising in his consciousness of a knowledge as to what to do in emergencies or in accidents, or when his body or the body of someone else was in great suffering. All the while there may also have been a tendency to want to be out in the open country close to orchards, or to fields of wheat, or among grapevines, or where the farmers were at work. There may have been in his consciousness a desire to know something of herbal extracts and of chemistry, and it would have been said of him probably that he was a youth of strange nature or temperament and tastes in his lines of study. But after being entered into the army as a young man, and after developing an appreciation of military training and regulation, new features were added to his character and personality so that when the time came for transition again, many new and valuable lessons of life had become established in his personality as guides and laws.

Therefore, we would find that when this man came into in his present incarnation his undeveloped personality consisted only of the deeply seated and unawakened elements of personalities from the past. Had there been any way of analyzing his past or scrutinizing the undeveloped personality residing within him as a boy of twelve or less we would have found that in that soul of his being his personality was like an unfinished book upon the pages of which were written certain laws and principles to become the fundamentals of his present personality.

We would have found the love for the country, the admiration of nature's processes, the instinct to save and to economize, the ability to plant and make things grow, the desire for greater knowledge and more modern advantages, the liking for chemistry and botany, the sympathetic feeling toward those who suffer, with a natural ability to know what to do to relieve such suffering, the instinct to live properly so as to guard against disease, and, with all, an inherent love of country and a highly developed degree of patriotism, and an instinctive dread of ammunitions, firearms, or physical conflicts. Out of this group of character elements, which the expert would call *complexes*, there developed gradually in the youth the natural desire to be engaged in some constructive, peaceful, conservative, modern, practical activity, which would entail no destruction of life, no sacrifice of personal needs, no lack of opportunity for education, and at the same time allow the expression of sympathy and the desire to help those who suffer.

Understanding, then, what were the essential elements of his evolved personality and what were the fundamental laws of his character, we should not be surprised to find that as he passed from one occupation to another in his present incarnation he finally found satisfaction and contentment in the service of a company devoted to the making of proprietary remedies from herbal extracts for the alleviation of physical conditions. In other words, we find him now as general manager of a company manufacturing and selling bottled extracts which are used by physicians and chemists in the preparation of remedies for physical suffering. In this business he has found opportunity to be in sympathy with all of the instincts of his nature and to express all of the complexities of his personality. He not only has found happiness in his work but an unusual degree of efficiency and expertness in his activity.

We would also understand from our study of his past why it is that in his present incarnation he had some "peculiar" whims or fancies, as his friends called them, and why he used to love to get away from the busy city life, with all of its tinsel and noise and rapid activities, and go out into the country and go among the orchards and the fields of growing things to ponder over the wonders of nature. We would also know why he loved to hear military music, loved to see the soldiers on parade, but had an inherent and well-fixed conviction that war was a brutal and unnecessary thing. And we would understand why, in his wealth and assured position of steady financial income, he still gave expression to some strange instinct of husbandry and insisted upon buying large supplies of essential goods and storing them in storerooms of his home, regardless of the fact that in these modern days all these supplies could be quickly purchased at nearby stores. These and many other traits of personality which seem to be inconsistent with that of a modern, conservative businessman would be called *complexes* by the student of character, and would be classified as *peculiarities* by relatives and friends.

Thus, this hypothetical man would be, today, the aggregation of his previous personalities. In his normal convictions he would exemplify those principles which had become convictions in character through bitter lessons of the past. In his ethical standards he would practice those things which he had learned were the best policies and principles. The weaknesses which this man might evince would represent tendencies which had not been modified by previous experience, and were, therefore, unaffected by lessons which had brought convictions and established principles. These weaknesses he would indulge in until by experience he had learned of their value or of their detriment in his life. In this way he would learn either to modify them or eliminate them so that by the close of his life these weaknesses would be overcome, or, if found pleasurable and non-injurious, would be continued as desirable elements of character for the future.

Each one of us is, in the same manner, an aggregation of our past personalities. In this life we draw upon the great lessons and experiences of the past and express them as the fundamental elements of our present character, while at the same time learning, through lessons and experiences, new principles and new elements out of which we decorate and modify, shade, blemish or improve *the beauty of our character.* This is the purpose of reincarnation. By its principles we are enabled to taste all of the cup of life and to learn all of its lessons. By our own will we overcome those things which are evil, eliminate those things which are detrimental, strengthen those things which are good, and thus perfect our ego and bring us close to the divine consciousness and the image of God.

In no other way can the human personality develop and evolve in *one span of life* on earth, even though it be of a hundred years. One span of life would be insufficient and inadequate in the time element alone to permit of the development, evolution, and perfection of a personality; and aside from the time element there are also the elements of human contact, environment, geographical location, varied occupation, and the progressiveness of civilization. Those born this year and living only a hundred years in the present time and never having lived before, and never to live hereafter, could not possibly evolve and develop a perfect personality of universal knowledge, experience, and understanding, for they would have no appreciation of the past through which man has developed and they would have no appreciation of the magnificent developments of the future.

To claim, therefore, that each soul *has but one short span of life on earth,* and that this span, separated from all the experiences of the past with their very valuable lessons, and separated from the magnificent lessons to be learned in the future, and in contact with only one phase of humanity in one country in one age of time, constitutes all that is necessary for a man or woman to develop and perfect a human character is absurd and unsound, as well as unfair and unjust.

If we, as human beings, are to be judged later on by the development and attained perfection of our characters, and by that judgment condemned eternally to peace or happiness, joy or sorrow, rich reward or eternal condemnation, then it is manifestly unfair that we should be born but once, handicapped and blighted by the original sins of our fore-bears and the great sin of Adam, and given but a few years under predestined conditions to accomplish those changes in our lives and characters which would eliminate all of the inherited sins and make us competent to overcome the sins of today and be ready for eternal judgment.

In fact, there would be no purpose served by the soul's entrance into a physical body for just one incarnation of a few short years. To be judged, therefore, because of the unattained perfection which is not possible in one incarnation is an injustice of such nature that it is incompatible with our beliefs in divine goodness, love, and mercy.

CHAPTER 11

THE RELIGIOUS AND BIBLICAL VIEWPOINT

Those who hesitate to accept the doctrines of reincarnation generally claim that no support for such doctrines can be found in any of the Western world religions. Those who are of the Christian denomination are especially positive in their statements that the Christian Bible, and the Christian doctrines as propounded by Jesus, contain no references to reincarnation and no statements which even tolerate, let alone support, the idea of reincarnation.

These persons argue that because some of the modern religions in the Western world, representing only a minority of the religious thought of the entire world, contain no support of the doctrine of reincarnation, that it should be rejected. In their minds the modern religions are the standard by which all others are to be gauged, and the beliefs of the minority are to supplant the beliefs of the majority. Such an attitude is a continuation of the ancient attitude of intolerance toward the truths held by others, and we are happy to find that in recent years the average person of the Western world is no longer inclined to be bound by the doctrines and beliefs of his forebears, but seeks knowledge and truth, regardless of its antiquity, its origin, or the fact that it may be incompatible with the creeds and dogmas of a minority of the Western civilization.

Fortunately, however, the belief that the religions of the Western world, and the Christian Bible, give no support to the doctrines of reincarnation is disproved by a careful analysis of available sources of indisputable information. Those who have heretofore held to the belief that the Occidental religions and those which constitute the religions of Western civilization contain no reference to reincarnation will be surprised by the facts I am about to give.

Before proceeding to quote from the standard versions of the Christian Bible, I feel that it is proper to explain why the doctrine of reincarnation is not generally recognized in the Western world as an almost universal religious belief. The two great religions of the Western world today are the Jewish and the Christian. The latter is fundamentally an outgrowth of the former. There are many eminent scriptural and religious authorities who claim that many of the theological principles of Christianity are founded upon mystical principles contained in the Oriental religious philosophies. We are safe in saying, however, that except for those new and unique doctrines taught by Jesus, the greater part of the Christian religion is similar to the Jewish religion, and in the Jewish religion one may trace very easily many principles of Oriental philosophies, which were found to be sound and useful, and which were retained by the Christian church during the processes of evolving the present-day Christian religion.

Before one can thoroughly understand all of the passages in the Christian Bible, as we find them in the standard versions, one must have some understanding of the religious beliefs which were universally accepted by the Jewish people at the time of the public preachings of Jesus. Many of the passages in the New Testament, and many of the references by Jesus to conditions existing around him, are not understandable unless one is familiar with the customs, habits, beliefs, and general philosophy of the people of his time. The passages in the New Testament referring to marriage and to the separation of the classes of people, and to the methods of praying, or the giving away of worldly things in order to become humble, are not fully appreciated by the Bible student, unless he is familiar with the customs, habits, and beliefs of the Jewish race at the time these allegorical or moral and ethical statements were made.

The moment the student of the Jewish religion and Jewish history becomes acquainted with the customs and habits of the people at the time of Christ's mission, he realizes that there are many interesting facts connected with the life of the people and their beliefs and general practices not elaborated upon in either the Old or New Testaments of the Bible, because they were so commonplace and so generally accepted and acknowledged that the writers of the Bible did not feel that it was necessary to comment upon them.

In many places in the Bible reference is made to stoning a person to death. No explanation is offered by any of the writers of the Bible as to why this method of punishment was universal in Palestine, for the writers probably believed that in their day when these facts were written, everyone was familiar with the history and universal nature of such a process. When one comes to study the history of Palestine and is fortunate enough to visit the country and live among the people for a while, one comes to realize that because of the abundance of small stones or rocks everywhere and the ease with which a multitude or a mob assembled at almost any place could reach down and quickly seize many rocks to throw at a person, that it was only natural for the mob practice of throwing stones to become a popular method. There are other references in the Bible to time of the day, periods of the year, seasons, climatic conditions, social practices, personal customs about the home, and other intimate facts which are not elaborated upon or explained in detail for the same reason.

Many of the important details about the crucifixion of Jesus the Christ are not given in the various accounts found in the New Testament simply because at the time that these accounts were written, the authors knew that the populace was familiar with such details and there was no reason for elaborating upon them in their accounts and, therefore, they dealt in detail with those points which were unique in connection with this historical event. For instance, the precise shape of the cross, the manner in which it was made, the manner in which the body was attached, and the manner in which the cross was erected, are points which were so familiar to everyone that comment upon them seemed unnecessary. There are thousands of similar voids of detail throughout the Bible which today are of great importance.

Because certain facts are not elaborated upon in the Bible is no reason for the student to believe that they did not exist or were not known to the mass of people. It may be safe to argue that since we find no reference in many ancient works to ice, that this form of frozen water was then unknown to the people of Palestine or elsewhere.

Historical research and scientific knowledge support our conclusion that ice may not have been known to the mass of people at that time in the sense we understand "ice" today.

But to argue that the art of dentistry was unknown because there is no reference in the Bible to artificial or false teeth is to make a serious mistake, inasmuch as research has proved that among the early Egyptians the art of dentistry was known, and many mummies have been found with artificial teeth. Likewise, no one should argue that no scientific or hygienic attention was given to childbirth simply because there is no reference to it to be found in the Bible, and because the most important birth recorded therein lacks any details regarding the attention given to the mother and child.

We now know that there were hospices for the care of mothers at delivery and that even the poor had attention voluntarily given by midwives or those who were capable of assisting at such a time. Because the details in this regard are lacking in connection with the birth of Jesus, it is not right to assume that Mary and Jesus had no hygiene or other professional attention. The authors of the story of the birth were not concerned with the facts that were commonly recognized as prevalent and general, but with those facts that were unique and of distinct importance.

The doctrine of reincarnation was generally accepted and universally established among the philosophers and mystics of the Jewish people at the time of the birth of Jesus and throughout his entire life, as we shall see in passages to be quoted. But this doctrine was not a purely religious one any more than the doctrine or principles associated with the conception of human life, and the birth of the human body, or the principles connected with the preparation of food, the curing of disease, or the preparation of the body for burial. Such commonly accepted and generally known principles were looked upon by the writers of the Bible as universal knowledge and had no more place in the scriptural writings than had the details of the planting of seeds in the ground for crops or the weaving of cotton into cloth, the sewing of costumes, the making of shoes, or the thousand and one other things that were part of the general knowledge, practice, and customs of the day.

There are many references, however, in the Christian Bible to the doctrine of reincarnation, which are positive, definite, and unquestionable, but they are associated with other statements in such a casual way that the average reader of the Bible overlooks them. This I will show later on where such passages are quoted. To prove, however, how universal was the belief in reincarnation among the Jewish people and among the disciples of Jesus, and even with Jesus himself, I am going to outline here some of the principal points in connection with reincarnation as held by the Jewish people during the Christian era. The same beliefs were also held by the people in the Oriental lands, but since the Christian and other present-day Western religions evolved out of the Jewish religion, we will limit ourselves to the presentation of the doctrines of reincarnation as known to and taught by the Jewish teachers. It is probably the first time that this information has been completely revealed in the Western world in connection with the subject of reincarnation.

I believe that I can do no better than quote from the precise words written within recent years by Moses Gaster, Ph.D., Chief Rabbi of the Jewish Congregation of London, and Vice-President of the Royal Asiatic Society, who is a widely recognized author on various subjects of Jewish religion, belief, and practice. The following paragraphs are condensations of his writings without comment. Remember that this eminent authority is referring wholly to Jewish beliefs and religious practices, and that he is quoting from such standard Jewish sacred books as the Zohar, the Manasseh ben Israel, and others.

*　　*　　*

The belief in the migration (or reincarnation) of the soul presupposes the existence of the soul; and a whole Esoteric system about the creation of the soul, and the conception of sin and redemption, are the fundamental principles upon which such a doctrine must rest. God is the creator of everything; therefore, souls are His creation. His creation came to an end with the close of the sixth day. At the beginning, the souls were created. The power of God is thus limited to what He had done on that occasion. The souls created, then, are of a limited number, as the creation was only a limited act, and had to come to an end at a definite period of time. These souls are God's *creation,* not any emanation from God. They are conceived as having an individual existence; they live separately and fully conscious of their individuality; they dwell in the heavenly halls or in paradise in rapt contemplation of the divine glory; thither they are allowed to return at the end of their peregrination through the lower world. The souls of the born and the unborn, of those who have already been in the earth world and of those who have not yet been in that world, are dwelling together in the heavenly halls or in the treasury of God (see Deuteronomy 32:34).

Moses in his ascent to heaven saw the souls of the great and pious and of those who have lived upon earth and of those who are to come to life hereafter—among others David and Aqiba. No new souls are created for each child that is born, the number of souls being limited. Man must by his actions approach the Divine, and his whole life must be a long sustained hymn of praise to God. But man, made of the dust of the earth, cannot rise to such perfection unless the Divine Soul lifts him up, and unless the Divine Law guides him steadily upward towards heaven. His life is a constant struggle between the grossly material inclinations inherent in his earthly nature and the high spiritual promptings of his Divine Soul. According to the way in which he inclines, his soul will become more or less contaminated by the contact with matter; it will lose more and more of its spiritual luster and purity. For man has absolute free will; he is master over his own actions.

The souls have been created for a specific use; they must enter human bodies; but the choice is not left to them, either of the bodies to be selected or of the time of entry, and the time and manner of exit. Although the soul forgets most of its spiritual existence when it enters into a body in the earth world, yet a dim recollection remains, a subconscious image, which is the guiding principle in elementary recognition of good and evil. Thus every man has within himself a standard of right and wrong given to his soul in its premundane existence. In the Zohar the incarnation of the soul is described in the following manner: All souls were created at the beginning of all creation; when not incarnated in bodies they dwell in heavenly bliss and divine illumination. When a body is being prepared to receive a soul, a soul requiring special earthly experience is directed or attracted to such a body as will provide such experience and knowledge. The law says unto the soul: "Ye shall see how the Lord has mercy on you. He has given you His precious pearl, the law, to help you in this world, so that ye may return pure." Thus the soul is given an opportunity through incarnation to compensate for its sins and purify itself, and thus rise one degree higher toward the ultimate perfection.

Now the soul begins it course upon earth. It must endeavor to obtain the absolute mastery over the body and not to become its slave. In the first entry, the soul is absolutely pure and without blemish. It is not met by the obstacle of original sin. The principle upheld always is that "Each man dieth by his own sin," but the weakness inherent in matter soon makes itself felt, and there are temptations placed in its way through the envy and spite of evil minds, which are anxious to drag it down to their own level. Through trial and trouble, man must win the crown of eternal bliss. A term is set for man's redemption. When all souls have thus become purified through successive reincarnations and have attained the ultimate goal of perfection, the kingdom of heaven upon earth will then be established. The evil in the world strives in vain to impede the steady development and unfolding of the evolving and purifying souls. The evil may delay the development of souls, but cannot indefinitely frustrate it. The soul, which has been contaminated through earthly experiences, can be purified again; the sins committed can be atoned for through compensation and even here the means is given to the soul to achieve its own purification. The soul retains its own consciousness and is sensible to its own failings; it realizes the bitterness of punishment and the tragedy of not being allowed to ascend on high and stand before God in its Pristine purity. After transition, it remains in an intermediate state of the spiritual world waiting an opportunity to purify itself and compensate for its sins. This comes to it by being re-embodied or reborn, and thus the soul migrates from one body to another. It may or may not remember in each incarnation its former existence. Such migration continues until all the blemish has been eliminated. Such migration of souls is made to serve another and still higher and more direct purpose—the Justice of God.

The great problem which has haunted every form of religious belief has been: how to reconcile the happiness of the sinner and trials and sufferings of the pious and good with the justice of God. Every religion has endeavored to establish a doctrine which would answer this question. Some of them have relegated the solution of this problem to a continued life after death, whereby the soul remains in combination with a physical body in order that the latter may suffer the torment of hell. Such an explanation was after all a subtle way out of a difficulty and it is not quite free from a possible reproach of selfishness. Not so with the belief in the reincarnation of the soul. Here, upon earth, in the sight of all, the sinner—whosoever he might be—has to expiate his sins. Here he has to suffer for the wrongs committed, and here obtain, as it were, a pass for the heavenly regions. By this slow process of purification in successive reincarnations the whole world would benefit and the general progress and welfare of mankind would be hastened.

There are, as it were, successive incarnations for each pre-existing soul, and for their sakes the world was created. Simon Magus put forth the claim of former existence, his soul passing through many bodies before reaching that known as Simon. The Samaritan doctrine of the *Taheb* teaches the same doctrine of a pre-existing soul, one of which was given to Adama, but which through successive incarnations in Seth, Noah, and Abraham, reached Moses. The doctrines further taught that not only is the world perfected by the rebirths of souls but each sinner gradually expiates his sin in this world in the new existences in which his soul reappears. The sinner's soul may enter the body of a pious man, and by his good deeds, he will cleanse the dross, still adhering to the soul, and facilitate its ascent on high. If a truly pious person suffers, it is only and solely because of sins committed in a previous incarnation and his suffering is not a punishment for sins *now* committed but a form of purgatory for evil deeds in a *former* life. Likewise the sinner benefits from the good deeds that he has performed in a previous existence whereby he may prosper now for a while, but if he continues to sin, he will absorb all of the good benefits from his past life and bring upon him suffering and punishment here or in his next incarnation.

There is a difference of opinion as to how many times a soul will reincarnate before it has attained perfection. It is generally believed that the full cycle of reincarnations is that in which the soul has performed the whole of the 613 commandments of the Law, by which alone perfection is attained. By means of reincarnation the soul fulfills the object of its creation—to pass through human existences on earth and to lift man higher and to bring him nearer the Divine. This doctrine, being a justification of God's ways with men, is, at the same time, a source of comfort to the pious, and a source of terror to the sinner. It reconciles man to suffering and trial, and at the same time explains the hidden meaning of many a law and ceremony which seems obscure.

* * *

The foregoing gives us an excellent idea of the general beliefs regarding the soul and its purpose in the world as popularly held by the mass of people in all of the Oriental countries. These beliefs were firmly fixed in the minds of the majority of men and women during the lifetime of Jesus and this being the case, we can understand better the many references made to this doctrine in the Christian Bible. In a later chapter I will refer to some of the specific points outlined in the foregoing picture of Jewish beliefs.

CHAPTER 12

CHRISTIAN REFERENCES

To those who are devoted to the Christian religion and who judge any moral, ethical, or religious doctrine by its compatibility with the writings in the Holy Bible, I now direct my attention.

In fairness to the subject, I plead with these devout Christians to be tolerant and liberal in their attitude for the time being, and consider the following remarks with the same degree of fair and just interpretation as they expect of others when they argue their beliefs and their principles of faith.

As stated in the previous chapter, there are many passages in the Christian Bible which directly and indirectly refer to reincarnation, and even Jesus the Christ referred to the doctrine of reincarnation in a manner which leaves no doubt as to his familiarity with the doctrine and his belief in it. The fact that the doctrine is not elaborated upon or explained in detail in the Bible is not a reason for concluding that it was not a popular doctrine or was one that was not acceptable to Jesus and his disciples.

The doctrine of reincarnation had no important place in the great message which Jesus brought to the world, and there was no more need for the presentation of the details of the doctrine in the writings of the apostles or the great prophets than there was for the presentation of the details of many other universally accepted scientific convictions and philosophical beliefs.

There is nothing in the doctrine of reincarnation that is not compatible with the doctrines expounded by Jesus, nor with the life he lived. I have shown in the previous chapters that the doctrines of reincarnation were universally known and accepted among the Jewish people and this fact was known also to Jesus. The belief in reincarnation, however, could not possibly prevent anyone from accepting the new messages expounded by Jesus, and there was no reason, therefore, for him to either criticize, modify, or comment upon the doctrine of reincarnation during his missionary work.

What Jesus said of the soul of man and of its redemption and salvation in nowise conflicts with the fundamental principles and great truth of reincarnation.

The average Christian believes that *somewhere* in the Bible, and *somewhere* in the sayings attributed to Jesus by his disciples, there is some statement regarding the soul to the effect that at transition the soul of man separates itself from the physical body and rises to a spiritual kingdom and there dwells in unconscious bliss or peace awaiting the ultimate Judgment Day. These persons also believe that Jesus, or his disciples, definitely stated that the soul of man after transition remains eternally in a spiritual kingdom, and that the Judgment Day will come when all have passed through transition and all are ready to be judged at one time. If these statements of Jesus were actually expressed in the Bible, they would certainly appear to be incompatible with the doctrines of reincarnation. But the fact of the matter is that no such statements were made by Jesus.

The idea that the soul of man leaves the physical body at transition to live eternally in a spiritual kingdom, awaiting

Judgment Day, is a doctrine that was *added to the Christian faith long after the life of Jesus,* and is not based upon anything said by him. Truly, there is reference to *judgment,* and to the dwelling of the soul in a spiritual kingdom, and of the ultimate and final weighing of our sins, but there is no statement to the effect that each individual may not have many incarnations before the time of the ultimate Judgment. The doctrine of reincarnation includes the coming of a final Judgment, and explains *how* and *why* we are given opportunities to prepare for that Judgment: but there is no reason to be found in the original teachings of Jesus to warrant the belief that at transition each soul of each individual passes to a spiritual kingdom, or any kingdom, where it must reside until the end of time awaiting the ultimate Judgment Day.

If the Christian or the student of Christian theology can honestly and bravely eliminate from his consciousness and from his categorical beliefs the idea that the soul of man at transition enters into a place or condition where it is to remain unto the end of time, then there will be no difficulty in accepting the true doctrines of reincarnation.

It will be seen that I am making a distinction between the Christian doctrines as taught by Jesus and propounded by his disciples, and the Christian doctrines which were *invented* or *agreed upon* by church conclaves in *later* centuries. I frankly admit that the present-day Christian doctrines as taught in the average Christian church do not permit of an acceptance of the doctrine of reincarnation. But these doctrines *are not the original doctrines of Jesus the Christ.* I am not attempting to criticize the goodness, or soundness, of the doctrines thus invented or adopted, except to state that they have included certain beliefs that are now contrary to reincarnation; but they are also contrary to the other passages in the Bible, as I will show by quotations. In other words, it is possible for a person to be a devout Christian and a sincere follower of the Lord Jesus Christ as man's savior, and as one of the Holy Trinity, and at the same time accept the doctrines of reincarnation. There are hundreds of prominent Christian clergymen and Christian advocates in America today who are firm believers in the doctrine of reincarnation and who do not find this ancient doctrine incompatible with anything taught by Jesus or anything demonstrated in his life.

To start our Bible research and investigation, let us turn to the Old Testament for just one of the many passages which clearly indicates the popular belief in man's continued rebirth. We will turn to the thirty-third chapter of the book of Job and proceed to read the last part of this chapter. Beginning at the twenty-seventh verse we find the belief of repentance and redemption expressed in clear language. We find the idea conveyed that if a sinful person confesses his sin at the time of transition or when he feels that his earthly life is about to end, he will save himself from future punishment and redeem his soul from the pit of darkness. In the twenty-eight verse we read that such a repentant sinner "will deliver his soul from going into the pit, and his life shall see the light." In the next verse we find the principles of reincarnation or rebirth expressed in these words, "Lo, all these things worketh God oftentimes with man." In the thirtieth verse there is a further explanation of the twenty-ninth verse. It reads: "To bring back his soul from the pit, to be enlightened with the light of the living."

Taking these three verses together there is no possibility of mistranslation or misunderstanding. Bringing the soul back from the pit into the light of the living can only mean one thing. The use of the word *pit* to mean the ancient burial places is a quite common expression in the Old Testament. It is often used to refer to the underworld or to Hades. The use of the word to indicate a grave or the place of the dead is shown in Ezekiel 32:23, Isaiah 38:18, Isaiah 14:15, and also in Job 33:18 we read of *the pit* as associated with death. To be redeemed from *the pit,* therefore, and brought back into the "light of the living," and to have this thing occur "oftentimes with man" can only mean being reborn after death and *given life again among the living.*

The thoughts expressed in these verses are reflected in many verses throughout both Testaments, as, for example, in Revelation: "Him that overcometh will I make a pillar in the temple of my God, *and he shall go no more out."*

When we start to analyze the New Testament we find that the same thoughts were held by the populace.

That Jesus was thoroughly familiar with the doctrine of reincarnation and of the law of compensation is made manifest in many of his statements. I am not going to take the time to quote every one of the statements made by Jesus to his disciples which would indicate this, but I will take one that is typical. In the Gospel of St. John in the ninth chapter, from the second to fourth verses, we find a very interesting incident that deals exclusively with reincarnation and the Law of Karma. In this instance Jesus passed along the highway with his disciples and met a man who was blind and who was known to have been born blind. The disciples considered this an opportunity to learn more about the Law of Karma and the cause of human suffering, and so they called the attention of Jesus to the blind man and asked:

"Master, who did sin, this man, or his parents, that he was born blind?" Jesus answered, "Neither hath this man sinned nor his parents: but that the works of God should be made manifest in him."

You will notice that the disciples distinctly stated that *the man was born blind,* and, therefore, they were puzzled as to the cause of the blindness. If his blindness had come about later in life through accident, injury, disease, mistreatment of the eyes, or through any of the many causes of blindness, there would have been no problem about his case. Please note that the question of the disciples was whether the blind man himself had sinned or his parents. If the parents had sinned, disease or accident might have been responsible for the man being born blind, but in what manner could the man himself have sinned to have brought about blindness *before birth?* Only by having sinned *in a previous life,* and by bringing the blindness upon himself as a karmic condition. No other interpretation can be given to this question on the part of the disciples.

Please note, also, that the disciples asked this question without hesitation and without apparent timidity. The question is stated as though it were a common question and a most natural one, and the very nature of the question itself indicates that the disciples were thoroughly familiar with the laws of Karma and rebirth, and that they knew that Jesus was familiar with rebirth and Karma as universal laws.

Note also that the answer given by Jesus is not a rebuke to their question, and is not a criticism of the beliefs held by the disciples, nor does it ignore the thoughts in the minds of the disciples which prompted the question. Jesus accepted the implication in their question and answered that neither the man nor his parents had sinned, but that the condition had come upon the man in order that God might teach a lesson and manifest a principle.

Certainly this one incident should be sufficient to show that Jesus and his disciples were thoroughly familiar with the doctrines of reincarnation or rebirth and Karma, and there was nothing repugnant, repulsive, or incompatible with the teachings of Jesus in the doctrine of reincarnation or Karma; otherwise, Jesus immediately would have corrected his disciples for expressing ideas along such lines and would have rebuked them for such erroneous thoughts. Throughout the New Testament we find that Jesus never missed an opportunity to correct his disciples or rebuke any one of them when he wrongly expressed a universal law or expressed a false principle.

In the third chapter of St. John, in the verses three to nine, we find another incident which clearly refers to the rebirth of the soul. Here Jesus is telling how important it is for a man to be born again in order that he may enter the Kingdom of God. Nothing is said as to how many times or how often a person must be reborn so as to purge the being of its sins and attain that purification which would admit one to the spiritual kingdom. But we find in the eighth verse of this chapter that the spirit, or soul, of man will come and go as the wind, and no one can tell how often or in what direction or in what manner it will come and go. This is an allegorical statement of the birth and rebirth of the soul, and the entire process of purification and redemption.

Another very pointed reference to reincarnation is found in the ninth chapter of St. Mark. Beginning at the eleventh verse we find Jesus again discussing, confidentially, the important doctrines of life with his disciples. The disciples were asking their usual questions and Jesus was answering in his typical manner. They asked him why the scribes were saying that Elias must first come. Jesus answered them and said that truly enough Elias would come first and restore all things but, he added, *Elias indeed has come.* The question as to the coming of Elias referred to his rebirth and to his coming again.

In the twelfth verse of the seventeenth chapter of St. Matthew the answer given by Jesus is amended slightly to include the fact that although Elias did come again as had been expected, the public knew him not and therefore disbelieved in him and mistreated him. In all of the references to Elias throughout the four gospels we find that the rebirth of Elias was expected. Nowhere did Jesus correct his disciples for expressing such an idea, but on the contrary, answered their questions and remarks with perfect compliance to the intimated principles of reincarnation.

We find this reference to the rebirth of Elias in one other very remarkable verification of the doctrine of reincarnation in the Holy Bible. I refer to that outstanding event recorded by Matthew, Mark, and Luke. Turning to the sixteenth chapter of Matthew we find that when the disciples were alone with Jesus again he wondered regarding the attitude of the public toward his life and his mission. He knew that they had expected the rebirth of Elias, and that every great avatar or son of God was considered a *reborn son of divine appointment.* Therefore, he wondered which of the expected reborn holy men the populace thought he was. So, he turned to his disciples and said, "Whom do men say that I, the Son of man, am?" In other words, he said to them, "Now that I am being discussed and talked about as the Messiah, who do they say that I am, since I am a son of man and am performing these so-called miracles and proclaiming these new teachings? In their conversations and in their private conferences, who do they say I really am?"

This question can refer to nothing else than the commonly discussed subject of rebirth and reincarnations. The public believed that he was a son of man, and that Joseph was his father or had accepted Jesus as his son, and there was no question in the minds of the populace as to who Jesus was *in his physical form* or hereditary lineage. Furthermore, Jesus would not have been concerned with such matters, and would never have asked such an inane question as, "Whose son do the people think I am?"

Notice the answer as given in the fourteenth verse. The disciples replied and said, "Some say that thou art John the Baptist; some, Elias; and others, Jeremias, or one of the prophets." Observe that the answers of these disciples referred to persons *who had been anticipated by rebirth* and who were expected to be born again, and who were being looked for by the populace as *reborn prophets* and leaders. Their whole reply is an expression of their belief in rebirth and a reflection of the common belief in reincarnation.

Jesus had an opportunity here to rebuke or correct his disciples for their expression of reincarnation principles, but he did not do so. He seemed to agree with their beliefs, as he did in every other instance where the principles of reincarnation were stated in his presence. His very answer to them is an acceptance of their statement and an acceptance of the principles implied. For he turned to his disciples and said, "But who say *ye* that I am?" In other words, he said to them that, after having been associated with him and learning his doctrines, and having been taught the secret of his mission and place in life, who did they understand that he was. It was here that Simon Peter made his famous reply and said, "Thou art the Christ, the Son of the living God."

Jesus accepted this statement and charged his disciples with keeping his divine identity a secret, and allowing the multitude to look upon him as any one of the former great characters as they pleased to do. The same incident is reported in practically the same words in the eighth chapter of the book of Mark and in the ninth chapter of the book of Luke. The fact that the incident is related in the same terminology with the same ideas by three of the gospel writers proves that it is not an incident of little importance, and that no "accidental wording" of the thoughts could be responsible for the principles implied.

As a further illustration of the general popular belief in the rebirth of individuals, we find in the ninth chapter of Luke, beginning at the seventh verse, another interesting incident. In this story, Herod heard of the wonderful work being done by Jesus and he was perplexed, because it was commonly reported that this new great teacher was none other than *John reborn,* while others claimed it was Elias, or one of the other prophets, come to life again on earth to live through another incarnation of activity. Surely, when the rulers of the country, and the public generally, hold such beliefs and they are discussed with Jesus and he does not correct them, but answers their questions with a sympathetic understanding of their beliefs in reincarnation, we cannot claim that these doctrines were unknown, *or new,* in his time.

Taking the foregoing quotations as typical examples, we find that whereas nowhere in the statements of Jesus, as contained in the Bible, is there any remark on his part that is incompatible with the belief in the doctrine of reincarnation, or any statement that man is born but once, or that after transition he never returns to earth again; yet, on the other hand, many quotations show that Jesus and his disciples believed in the rebirth on earth. So we are forced to realize that those who object to the doctrine of reincarnation on the basis of its incompatibility with Christian beliefs are misled by the statements made by modern Christian leaders who cannot find authority for their statements in anything that Jesus said.

Returning to the one example of where the disciples asked Jesus, "Who sinned, this man, or his parents, that he was born blind?" we want to call attention to the fact that it was thoroughly understood among the Jewish people that the sins committed in a previous incarnation would bring about some form of punishment in this life. Let me quote again a paragraph from the Jewish doctrine of the time: "If a truly pious person suffers it is only and solely because of sins committed in a previous incarnation—a form of purgatory for evil deeds in a former life." This passage is from the writings of the eminent Jewish rabbi whom I have already quoted in this book. It was this point that aroused the inquiry on the part of the disciples.

Certainly there is no reason for devout Christians to feel that the doctrines of reincarnation, as presented in this book, are inconsistent with the fundamental principles of true Christianity, nor contrary to anything that Jesus taught or his disciples believed. We find in the foregoing few quotations sufficient proof of the acceptance of the doctrine of reincarnation on the part of Jesus and his disciples.

If the later Christian churches, or the modern Christian religion, have modified the pristine teachings of Jesus, or introduced new doctrines that are contradictory to those held by Jesus, no true Christian should feel that he is bound to accept them simply because they have the approval of modern religious authorities. For that matter, many of the modern Christian lights and leaders of Christian thought have accepted the doctrines of reincarnation and have publicly stated that these doctrines are the only just and fair explanation of the universal laws of life.

The doctrines of reincarnation, as set forth in this book, do not do away with redemption, salvation, and the ultimate judgment of our sins, nor do they set aside any of the fundamental principles that Jesus taught or which constitute the foundation stones of the Christian religion. Devout Christians who are sincere and tolerant in their examination of the Christian principles and sincerely striving to understand their religion better, will find in these doctrines a valuable aid in understanding life. The bigoted and prejudiced will simply close their eyes to the statements in this chapter of my book, and will attempt to explain away the quotations I have given in the belief that they conceal other thoughts or other ideas which we do not understand. Therefore, I will make no further attempt to prove that the doctrines of reincarnation are compatible with the beliefs and teachings of Jesus. The wise and fair-minded persons will be quite satisfied; the others can never become convinced by any rational argument.

CHAPTER 13

THE OVERSOUL AND CYCLES OF INCARNATIONS

It has been intimated in the preceding pages of this book that there is but one soul existing throughout the entire universe and this soul is the consciousness and divine essence of God. It has also been intimated that the so-called individual souls of human beings are not separate and independent souls, but *unseparated segments* of the Universal Soul, never losing their association or contact with this consciousness of God and the divine essence which constitutes the vital life force. Because these facts may be new to a great many Western minds it seems appropriate at this moment to augment these statements with the use of schematic diagrams and symbols, and make plain the beautiful fundamental laws which are involved in the principles set forth in this book.

That there is *one soul* in the universe, and that this soul is the consciousness and vital essence of God should not be surprising to any devoted student of sacred literature; nor will it be surprising to those who have made a careful study of the fundamental laws of biology and ontology.

If God is the creator of all things, and from his consciousness and divine essence emanates all consciousness and all vitality, then all consciousness throughout the universe and all vital energy of a living, creative nature must have *one central, divine source,* and must be continuous and uniform throughout the universe.

Even a moment's reflection will reveal that it is far more difficult to think of God having created out of his consciousness and essence millions upon millions of individual souls, each retaining its distinct individuality and separateness, than it is to think of *one universal essence and one universal* soul. To conceive of any means of maintaining individual entities of the same soul essence and same divine consciousness, without a tendency on their part to unite and blend into *one essence and one consciousness,* is a difficult thing indeed.

God, the creator of all things, is the Father of all images created by him in his likeness. We cannot conceive of the human children of one earthly father as being of a vital essence or blood energy so separated that the same essence is not in each of them. With the soul essence, however, we are dealing with a subtle and transcendental energy that pervades all space and which cannot be isolated or confined in any enclosure, and we cannot conceive of this essence as being in a human form without at the same time extending beyond that form and contacting the same essence resident in all other human forms.

When the sacred writings of the Orientals and even of the Christians speak of the soul in man, they do not necessarily imply an *individualized* and *separated soul,* but the *soul essence* and *soul consciousness* of God that is resident in man. Each of us has *soul,* but not a *soul* in the sense that it is a *thing apart from every other soul* in human beings.

To illustrate the principle, or law involved, I have resorted to the homely illustration of the electricity that is utilized in the lighting of modern electric lamps.

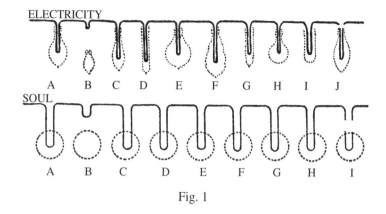

Fig. 1

In Figure 1, I have shown the electric wires in the upper part of the drawing passing along from lamp to lamp without any break in their connections. The lamps A, C, D, E, F, G, H, and I are various types of electric bulbs common in use today. Some of them are colored with various tints; some are very small and give only a small amount of light, others are large and very luminous; some are long, and some are short.

The electricity that flows into each *one* of these lamps, and causes the lamp bulb to be alive with light, is not broken in its continuity or in its flow through *all of the lamps.* The electricity that illuminates these bulbs and gives them life or *light* flows through each lamp and out again to enter into the next lamp, and so on. The electric current, therefore, in each lamp may be likened to the *soul essence* of the lamp, and while we would say that each lamp *has its own electricity* which it is utilizing, we cannot look upon that electricity in each lamp as *being separated from or distinct from the electricity that is in all of the other lamps.* Merely a *segment* of the electric circuit is resident in each lamp, and *all of these segments are united* in one continuous circuit. Even if we separate one of the lamps from the circuit, as shown at B in the diagram, the electricity that was once resident in the bulb comes to the point or place of its former entrance into the lamp bulb, and then passes on into the next one. The lamp that no longer has the electric current passing through it is now *lifeless and without light.*

In the lower part of Figure 1, I have compared the universal soul essence and consciousness with the electric current. The dotted circles labeled A, B, C, D, E, F, G, and H at the bottom of this diagram represent human physical bodies and the upper dark line represents the soul essence and consciousness of the universe, with segments of it coming down and passing through each of the physical bodies. You will see at once that this divine consciousness and essence, called *soul,* is not broken into *individual* and *separate* segments in each one of the physical bodies, but passes into each body and manifests there, giving the body life, yet manifests simultaneously in the other physical bodies. While the segment of soul is in one of these physical bodies it manifests consciousness, life, and intelligence in the physical body, and without this soul essence the physical body would be lifeless and without intelligence or consciousness. The dotted circle B represents a physical body after transition when the soul essence and consciousness have withdrawn from the body and left it lifeless and unconscious.

The electric lamp bulbs are not electric lights until electricity manifests in them and through them. When you buy an electric bulb at a store and carry it home with you, you have nothing more or less in your hands than some of the minerals of the earth, gathered together by a scientific process and formed into a body by the master creators of electrical devices. You cannot call it a *light*, since it manifests no light, and it is therefore lifeless, useless, and without any value so long as it is unassociated with the electric current. The moment you place this bulb in a socket, or in a position where the electric current can flow into it, you immediately transform the lifeless, lightless, physical body of the bulb into a *vibrating illuminating, living thing* of light, and the moment the electric current or electric essence is withdrawn from the bulb it is again lifeless and useless and cannot fulfill the purpose for which it was made.

Man's physical body is precisely like the electric bulb. Every bit of its physical and material form and nature has been extracted from the earthly elements and drawn together by a marvelous process and formed by a Master Creator, but until the divine essence of life and consciousness enters that physical body it is lifeless and truly lightless.

This recalls to our minds the principle that is so well worded in the Christian Bible, in the book of Genesis, wherein we are told that God formed man out of the dust or elements of the earth, and then breathed into his nostrils, or into his physical body, the *breath of life* or the divine essence, and man became a *living soul*. Until such essence was breathed into his body man was lifeless and incapable of fulfilling the purpose for which he was created, and he was of no more use than an electric light bulb before the electric essence gives it light and life. The physical body of man is without divine intelligence or consciousness, and without vitality or purpose, until the soul enters it and makes it a living soul rather than a mere existing body.

We can see by these two illustrations that the soul essence and consciousness resident in each physical body is not separated from the essence and consciousness that is in *every other living body.* If we were to think of the soul in each individual body being a *separate* and *distinct soul,* independent of all the others, and not in actual contact with all others, we would have a condition similar to that shown by the letter J in the upper part of Figure 1. Here the electric lamp bulb has the electric wires within it but these are not connected with the electric circuit. We see at once that a lamp in this condition is no different from that shown by the letter B, for there is no contact between the electric wires in the bulb and those which contain the real energy. Such a lamp could not manifest light of any kind.

By looking at the body identified as letter I at the end of the lower diagram, we see that same point illustrated by breaking the connection between the soul in the body and the universal soul essence. We see at once that such a condition is an impossibility, for the soul essence and the consciousness in a physical body must remain in contact with the *source of essence* and the *source of consciousness* in order to maintain its manifestation of essence and consciousness. Matter itself is not intelligent, for it is composed of the gross elements of the earth, and these elements have neither mind nor consciousness until they are organized and prepared to receive some form of consciousness.

Long ago the ancient philosophers and mystics gave a name to the universal soul and consciousness that pervades all space. This name we have modernized into the term *Oversoul.* Some have called it the Cosmic Soul; some have called it the Divine Soul; and others the Soul of God. Such other terms, however, imply that there are various kinds of souls in the universe, and that one of these is divine, or the *Soul of God* or of the Cosmic, whereas the others are not. But, since there is *but one soul* in the universe, the term *Oversoul* is preferred, because it does not attempt to distinguish this soul from any other, except to intimate that it is the soul that exists everywhere without being separated from its various manifestations in physical bodies.

Therefore, we will use the term *Oversoul* to mean the Universal Soul or God, or, in other words, the divine consciousness and essence of God which pervades all space, and segments of which are manifested in each human body. This means that in the body of each human being there is the soul essence, the power, the energy, the consciousness of God, that *God is within us* rather than without. This brings us to a clearer understanding of many of the sacred writings of the past and especially those which are found in the Christian doctrines.

In thinking of the Oversoul extending a part of itself downward and into the body of each human being, we must give some thought to the relationship of the soul to the ego and the personality of each human being, as touched upon in preceding chapters. In order to impress these relationships upon the mind of my reader I have resorted to another schematic illustration which is given here as Figure 2.

Here we have two heavy dark lines descending from above and coming down into a circular enclosure. Let us consider the two dotted circular lines in the center of the diagram as representing the physical body of man. Inside of these two dotted lines we see the heavy black lines representing the soul essence and consciousness descending from the Cosmic into the physical body. In the center of this soul we find another body, often referred to as the *psychic body,* which is the ego or personality, and this ego is composed of the mind and memory that is associated with each segment of the Oversoul.

In other words, if we look upon the Oversoul in the universe as being divided into unbroken segments, and each segment representing a part of the Oversoul that resides in a human body, we will find that each one of these segments of the Oversoul possesses an ego or personality composed of mind or intelligence, and consciousness with memory. The soul itself is composed of the divine essence, or vital life force—creative energy which emanates from God, the source of all life. However, in addition to this creative and vitalizing energy of the soul, each segment possesses, as an attribute, an ego or personality, with its mind, memory, and consciousness. As I have stated above, this ego or personality, with its divine mind and divine consciousness, has often been referred to as the *psychic body* of man, resident with in the physical body.

In Figure 2 you will also see the aura radiating from the physical body. This aura is like the radiations of light that come from an electric bulb when the wires within are connected with the source of electricity. The aura of the human body is the result of the soul essence and vitality resident within the physical body. I have illustrated this aura in the form of an egg or oval, inasmuch as the aura within a human body is often seen in this form, and in many ancient manuscripts the aura of man is referred to as an egg, and therefore symbolical of the reproductive energy of the ani-

Fig. 2

mal kingdom. When the soul with its essence and consciousness is withdrawn from the physical body, the aura follows the soul and no longer manifests around the physical body. As I have stated elsewhere in this book, thousands of observations have been made at the time of transition when the aura of the physical body has been seen to rise above the body and to remain in space as the soul withdrew and left the body lifeless.

It is very important that the elements of Figure 2 should be carefully studied. Keep in mind that the two black lines represent the divine essence of the Oversoul descending into the physical body. The physical body is represented by the two large dotted circular lines. But, the soul in the body has also other attributes besides its divine essence and vitality. These attributes constitute the ego or personality, with mind and memory. This ego or personality *always remains with each segment* of the Oversoul, for the ego is immortal like the soul itself, and cannot be destroyed and never ceases to exist. Whether the segment of the soul *is in the physical body* or *out of it*, the ego, with its mind, memory, and consciousness remains with it, and so we see that we can have an intelligent, conscious segment of the soul either *in a body* or *out of a body*. When it is *in a body* we have the union of the spiritual with the material, making a perfect manifestation of a living soul on earth. When it is *out of a body* we have a physical body that is lifeless, unintelligent, and unconscious, and a segment of soul still retaining its vitality and consciousness, ego, and intellect.

With these points well fixed in your mind we will now look at Figure 3. Here I have shown a number of physical bodies with the soul segment and personality, or ego, in them. A, B, C, and F represent living bodies with the soul essence and ego resident in them, and the aura of life extending around the physical body. At D, I have shown what occurs at the time of transition. Here the soul with its ego and aura is withdrawn from the physical body, leaving the body without any aura or life. At E, I have shown the complete separation, and you will notice that I have illustrated this by showing the segment of the soul still maintaining its aura and personality or ego, although having ascended into the Cosmic and no longer in contact with the physical body which is now lying into the dust of the earth, disintegrating and returning to its primary elements.

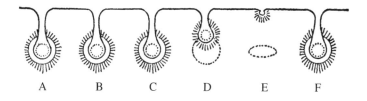

A   B   C   D   E   F

Fig. 3

You will notice by studying Figure 3 that all of the egos in each segment of the Oversoul are connected and associated through the contact with the divine soul essence, and that even in the case where the soul has completely withdrawn from the body, the ego of the segment is in contact with all of the other egos through its universal contact with the Oversoul.

So much for the illustration of the principle of the universal association and contact of all egos in all living things. This should impress us with the principle that the personality which each of us possesses throughout life, or the ego which we manifest throughout life, is not a *mortal* thing but an *immortal* thing, and a part of the Oversoul existing eternally.

We should also be impressed with the fact that the ego, or personality, which each of us manifests during our lifetime, continues to exist and retain its identity over after transition. Therefore, there are egos, or personalities, existing in physical bodies on the earth, and existing *outside of physical bodies* in the Cosmic. And all of these egos, or personalities, incarnated in bodies or existing outside of bodies in the Cosmic, are in contact and constant communication with each other through having the same soul essence continuously passing through them.

Incidentally, it may be mentioned that this ancient understanding of the association of all egos with each other, and the uniting of all souls into one *soul,* was the foundation for the belief in the *universal brotherhood of man* through the *universal fatherhood of all beings*, and establishes the fact that all human beings are brothers and sisters under one creator and of the same essence, same vitality, and same consciousness, regardless of race, creed, color, or other distinctive elements of the ego.

The next important consideration is in regard to the cycles of incarnations. The question its often asked as to how many times man incarnates on earth, and when this process of development will discontinue. Mysticism, and the scientific study of this subject, gives a well-known example of *perfect soul personality development,* whereby the need for further incarnations on earth was brought to an end. This is in the case of *Jesus the Christ,* who, having had many previous incarnations as intimated in the Christian gospels, was finally born pure and with a personality or ego requiring only *one more* group of experiences. At the end of these experiences, which were to demonstrate the highest principles of cosmic law and God's will and power, *Jesus the Christ* having attained Christhood through the highest perfection and pureness of a consciousness, ascended into heaven and was there absorbed into the consciousness of God, and the ego of Jesus became one of the divine elements of the Godhead.

Until such perfection is attained by each human being, there will be need for each personality and each ego to reincarnate *again and again,* and through the experiences of life, through personal effort and attainment, through devotion and sacrifice, purge the ego of all evil in thought or action, and finally become pure in every point and ready for the ultimate Judgment, when it will be accepted unto God again and become a part of the Divine Godhead.

Jesus himself promised that this would be the ultimate and highest reward for all devotion and effort toward godliness. What he stated in this regard was well understood by the prophets who preceded him, but none of whom had attained the degree of perfection attained by him.

Therefore, we see that it is impossible to tell how many times each ego, or personality, must be reincarnated in physical form on the earth plane. One point, however, in regard to the cycles of reincarnation, has been determined by observation. It has been found that each ego, or personality, reincarnates on earth *approximately every 144th year.* In other words, 144 years has been found to be the average length of time *between rebirths.* This does not mean, however, that there can be no exception to that average. Just as there is an average length of time for human gestations, although this may vary at times, so there is an average length of time between rebirths on earth, although this, too, may vary according to circumstances.

It has been found, however, that although there is a variation in these periods of 144 years, after ten or twelve reincarnations the number of years involved in them shows that the average time is about 144 years between rebirths in infant bodies.

Nominally, man should live in his physical body 144 years, and then the soul would withdraw from that body, ascend to the Cosmic, and in a few days, or few hours, descend again into a new body. But, man by his manner of living, and his continued violation of natural laws, has gradually shortened his length of time on earth so that the average physical body reaches transition long before 144 years have passed. But since he will not be *reborn again* until the 144th year, there will be a period of cosmic residence for his ego, during which the ego will await the coming of the 144th year of rebirth.

In other words, if a person lived to be 100 years of age on earth, and then passed through transition, the ego would have a period of waiting in the Cosmic for 44 years until the normal time for rebirth. If a person lived to be 124 years of age on the earth, the ego would wait in the Cosmic 20 years. And a person who had lived 80 years of earthly life would reside in the Cosmic for 64 years.

By referring to Figure 4, we will see these periods of re-births plainly illustrated. The top line of Figure 4 shows the cycles of rebirth divided by periods of 144 years. In this top lines the double circles labeled E, represent the *cycles of life on earth,* or, in other words, the cycles of the soul incarnated in a physical body. The small dotted circle above the line, marked with the letter S, represents the *spiritual residence* of the ego in the Cosmic. The entire top line shows an imaginary life line of an ego that lived *on earth 100 years* in each period, *and 44 years in the Cosmic* in each period. Starting with the first birth on earth we find that the next rebirth occurred at the 144th year, the second at the 288th year, the third at the 432nd year, etc. In other words, in 1152 years this personality would have passed through eight incarnations on earth and would be ready for the ninth.

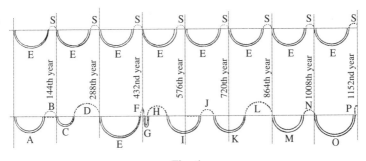

Fig. 4

Such an equal division of births and rebirths is purely imaginary, however, and probably impossible to find in actual experience. Therefore, let us consider the lower line of Figure 4. Here we have an imaginary life line of a person as we may find it in any part of the world. In this life line we soon notice that the periods of life *on earth* are of various lengths. Beginning at the start of the line we find that the first period on earth, indicated by the letter A, was about 90 years, leaving a period of 54 years for the personality to reside *in the Cosmic*, as shown by the dotted line B. At the 144th year, however, the personality was reborn on earth, and this rebirth is shown by the double line marked C. This period on earth, however, was for only 50 years, and after transition the personality resided on the cosmic plane for 94 years, as shown by the dotted line D.

Then, in the 288th year, the personality was reborn, as shown by the double line E. The earthly existence this time was for 135 years and the personality then ascended to the Cosmic and resided there for 9 years, as indicated by the dotted line F. At the end of this cosmic period the personality was reborn, as shown by the double line marked G, but this time the earthly life was for only 10 years, and after transition the personality ascended into the Cosmic; but because its previous period on earth *had been so short* the personality resided in the cosmic for only 35 years, and then was reborn, as shown by the double circle marked I.

Thus we see there were short and long periods on both the earth and cosmic planes, and the rebirths did not always occur at precisely the 144th year of the cycle. However, we notice that at the end of 1152 years this personality had passed through approximately eight incarnations on earth, just as had the imaginary one on the upper line of the diagram. Therefore, although one of these lives was not strictly according to the 144-year periods, it did average about eight incarnations to 1152 years.

So it has been found with the average person whose incarnations have been traced through past history. Although they have not always been reborn at precisely the 144th year of the complete cycle, nevertheless taking ten, twelve, or fourteen of the past incarnations and dividing the number of years involved by the number of earthly incarnations, we find that they did average about 144 years between rebirths.

A child born today and living but a few hours, and then passing through transition, may have its ego reside in the Cosmic for the balance of 144 years or it may be reborn in ten, twenty, or fifty years. But, after a number of reincarnations the average period will be found to be 144 years.

This means that the average person living today can roughly estimate that he or she was reborn approximately each 144-year period backward through history. The rule is not exact, for there are exceptions as shown in the lines of

Figure 4. Why some personalities are reborn sooner than others can only be judged by a consideration of the law of Karma. Since the purpose of the ego's residence in the Cosmic awaiting rebirth is to be purified and instructed, and prepared for the next incarnation, we may safely judge that those who have lived a pure and nearly perfect life here on earth up to the time of transition will require a very short time of cosmic preparation before being reborn. On the other hand, those who have fallen out of grace and who have yielded to temptation and who have sinned much will probably find that they must spend the full and allotted time upon the cosmic plane in being purged and prepared for rebirth.

We seen in all of this the marvelous and beautiful justice of God's ways, and of the uniformity of cosmic laws and principles manifested even in the cycles of life, as they are in the formation of crystals, the movement of planets, and the composition of the elements of matter.

Even man's life on earth is divided into periods and cycles of seven years each, during which certain definite things occur in the life of everyone. By a study of these earthly cycles any man or woman can easily foresee and foretell what definite events will occur in their earthly lives, and prepare for them, and take advantage of those which are propitious or fortunate. In my book dealing with the cycles of life* on earth, all of these periods have been explained and worked out in the tables, so that each and every person can easily determine the fortunate and unfortunate periods of his earthly life and be prepared for emergencies of all

---

*Self Mastery and Fate, With the Cycles of Life, published by the Supreme Grand Lodge of AMORC.

kinds. Even the cycles of previous incarnations can be determined in this way, and it is possible to learn what our previous personalities and egos manifested in our last incarnation. Since all of this has been dealt with exhaustively in my other book, I will not deal with it here, for it has no definite place in the discussion of the present subject.

CHAPTER 14

BETWEEN INCARNATIONS

Two questions arise as to the activities of the soul during its period of temporary existence in the spiritual realm between rebirths. The first of these is, Why should the soul have a long or short existence in the spiritual world between incarnations? The second is, What is known of the soul's activities in these periods between earthly incarnations?

The first question is generally associated with the thought that if it is advisable for the soul of man to have a number of successive rebirths on earth in order to develop and perfect the ideal ego, why does not the soul pass from one body at transition immediately to another without more than a few minutes or few hours elapsing between the two great events? In other words, why should there be any delay at all in the soul's passing from one body which it is vacating to the new body it is to occupy?

Considering that throughout the world there are births occurring every minute of the day and night it would seem that no matter when transition occurred with anyone, the soul could escape from the old physical body it occupied and pass immediately into another body just being born. There are many thousands of persons, having only a slight acquaintance with the doctrines of reincarnation, who believe that this often occurs. There are those who believe that when a mother passes through transition at the time of childbirth her soul passes right into the newborn body, not only because the body was close at hand and ready to receive a soul, but because of the relationship that exists. There are a great many who also believe that when an elderly person passes away in any community, the soul of that person will immediately enter the body of any child being born in that community.

These ideas are the result of a lack of knowledge of the principles involved, as outlined in the preceding chapter. Each personality or ego of the Oversoul has a definite cycle of rebirth with periods of spiritual existence between them. We have seen in the preceding chapter how the earthly incarnations of the soul, with its ego and personality, may vary in length from one hour to one hundred years or more, and how the periods between incarnations will vary in length; but only occasionally would there be a very brief or short period of existence in the spiritual realm between incarnations.

The purpose of these intervals between incarnations is to permit the ego to purify itself further and become illuminated by the Divine Mind and Cosmic Wisdom. It is like a period of rest and relaxation between hours of daily labor. It is refreshment for the soul and personality, and is strength to the spiritual powers of the divine faculties of the soul.

We may compare the intervals between incarnations to the hours of sleep that occur between the daytime periods of activity in our daily affairs. We may labor sixteen or eighteen hours of the day in waking consciousness and then spend from six to eight hours in sleep, wholly unconscious of our earthly objective affairs. These hours of sleep and rest afford an opportunity for the gathering of strength and recreation of the tired, worn-out, and exhausted faculties and functioning of the physical body. Sleep permits stronger exercise of the faculties and a more vitalized degree of power in the body and mind in the morning when the body awakens.

The same can be said regarding the intervals between incarnations. Immediately upon transition the soul and ego of the individual separate gradually from the body. This separation is not so sudden that the entire soul essence and ego are withdrawn from the body and rise *instantly* to the spiritual or cosmic realm. The withdrawal of the soul essence and ego from the body requires from ten minutes to a half-hour and sometimes more time. This has been observed in thousands of cases where in homes, hospitals, and sanitariums, persons have been gathered about the bedside of a person passing through transition, or where very observant nurses or doctors have made the notations.

Generally, when there is a soft light in a room, or other vibratory or magnetic conditions which are favorable, the aura of the human body will be seen to extend itself gradually as transition begins, and this aura of a very faint color or combination of colors will gradually rise out of and above the body, until, in from five to twenty minutes, it is almost wholly out and above the body, and separated from it. But it does not continue to rise and does not leave the presence of the body for some little time. In some cases the aura has been observed to remain in the same room, hovering over the body or near it for many hours; and in cases where the light of the room and other conditions were favorable for observation, this aura has been seen to continue in the presence of the body for several days.

In many cases perfect observation of the aura near the body after transition has been interfered with by the sudden lighting of many lights and the presence of persons who had to perform their proper duties in caring for the body. In cases where there was no such interference for hours the observation of the aura has been perfect, and many interesting details have been noted.

In many ancient writings this phenomenon has been commented upon. In those cases where the aura or ego of the body was seen to linger and remain in the presence of the body for several days (or in the room where the transition had occurred) it was claimed that the soul or ego was "earthbound."

The belief is quite common in Oriental lands, among people who have observed and studied the action of the soul after transition, that the soul and ego remains after the separation from the body to perform certain definite things before rising above the earth plane to exist in the spiritual realm. Among the purposes thus referred to are the soothing and strengthening of the principal mourners or those who have been suddenly and seriously affected by the transition, the inspiring of certain actions or thoughts in the minds of intimate associates, and the untanglement of many mysteries that might be connected with the transition.

It has been claimed, for instance, that hundreds of carefully studied cases show that where transition has occurred suddenly without giving the individual an opportunity to look after a serious problem and properly to advise those who would be left in a quandary, the soul or ego has remained in the immediate environment of the relatives or companions of the deceased and aided them by inspiration or intuition to locate certain papers, hidden valuables, or other matters of extreme importance. It is also claimed by these authorities that the ego often remains in contact with the mourners to point out to them through intuition, or otherwise, the cause of transition when this has occurred through murder or accident involving a serious mystery.

In many other ways the ego can have a very soothing and comforting effect upon those who were closest to the deceased. It is this record of carefully observed facts regarding the ego's contact with the earth plane after transition that gave rise to the superstitious belief in the existence of ghosts.

When the uneducated and uniformed minds heard of the instances of egos remaining for a while to point out how a crime had been committed, or where an accident occurred, or where certain papers and documents were concealed, they believed that the ego was a highly luminous figure of the deceased's body, and that it remained for an indefinite time in the environment of the transition and made itself visible to every person that came near the place where transition occurred. As I have said, this sort of belief was responsible for the development of the idea of ghosts which is so prevalent among the ignorant.

The truth of the matter is that only those whose psychic development or spiritual development has reached a high state can see the faint aura of the released soul and ego. Those who were closest to the deceased and who would be the most likely to receive any impressions from the ego very often do not see the lights of the aura, but feel the magnetic or vibratory radiations of the ego for many hours, or several days after transition, and they usually have a strong impression that the personality of the deceased is still in their midst trying to comfort and sympathize with them, and still lives.

The more sympathetic and complete the attunement that existed between the deceased and those who are left here on earth, the more perfect will be this impression of the ego's presence after transition, and this impression is unmistakably definite in the minds of mothers when a son or daughter, of a loving and companionable nature, has passed through transition.

It has been claimed by some students of this phase of universal principles that a man or woman who was given in earthly life to an exaggerated faith in material things was sure to be "earthbound" for some days or weeks after transition, and that the material things which enslaved him during his earthly life would continue to hold him to the earth plane for some little time. Thus they believed that a man who was a miser, or who gave his whole heart and mind to money or material wealth, or to some earthly thing which he made his God, would be bound and enslaved to this thing for many days or weeks after transition. In this wise came the expression that certain persons were doomed to be "earth-bound."

Many fantastic stories have been written with this idea as the principal theme, and there are many astute and successful criminologists in various lands who claimed that their experience in solving murder mysteries and some other crimes has proved to them that a person who committed murder or some very serious crime against an innocent person is "earthbound" by this crime and for days and weeks after transition will linger in the vicinity of the crime in an attempt to aid in the solution of the mystery. These persons claim that the ego finds no peace, no happiness, and no opportunity to rise and free itself from the earth, until it does assist in solving the mystery of the crime it committed and in seeing that no innocent person suffers for the crime that it committed. These criminologists claim that by waiting patiently and observing the action of other persons and analyzing the impressions that come to the minds of those formerly closely associated with the deceased, many clues will be found that will aid in solving the mastery.

This is a very wonderful field for exploration and study on the part of those who are interested in criminology, and in the possibilities of "earthbound" egos inspiring in the minds of others the correct solution of the crimes they have committed. Such a subject has no place in this work, even though many Rosicrucians in various lands have been delving deeply into this subject with eminent success.

Shortly after transition, however, the soul and ego are drawn upward into the spiritual or cosmic realm, and there remain until the time comes to descend again toward the earth plane to enter into a newborn body. As stated in the previous chapter, the personality or ego remains with the segment of the soul as a part of it, and the ego never loses its identity nor does the segment of the Oversoul associated with this ego ever lose its identity. Whether the ego is to remain in the spiritual realm for a week, a month, or many years depends upon various laws and principles with which we are not as familiar as we are with those laws and principles pertaining to the soul and ego's existence on this earth plane.

During its period of spiritual existence the soul with its ego and personality is in immediate contact with all of the minds and egos, not only in the spiritual realm, but throughout the universe. I have shown in the preceding chapter that at all times every soul expression and every ego in the universe, whether incarnated in a physical body or existing on the spiritual plane, is united and in continuous contact with all others because of the continuous contact of the Oversoul. This permits of the divine mind or psychic body of each ego communicating with every other psychic mind without difficulty.

The only manner in which the mind of the physical, outer self can know of such universal communications is by having the knowledge transferred from the inner self, or ego, to the outer self. In this very important point lies the one problem which makes universal communication seem either impossible or uncontrollable.

The untrained and the undeveloped experimenter in telepathy or in cosmic communications is apt to judge his ability to communicate with others by the degree of knowledge that is thus transferred from the inner self to the outer self. The outer self has no other way of knowing whether the inner self is ever in contact with other egos or not, except through the occasional transference of some impression from the inner self to the outer consciousness. If such transference or impressions is only occasional, or incomplete and indefinite, the outer self will misjudge the true functioning of the ego in this regard.

Experiments made by those who understand the laws and principles reveal that it is as easy for one ego to communicate with another as for one outer self to speak to another in a room. It has also been found that our inner selves are constantly receiving impressions from the Cosmic which have been released by other egos and that this sort of exchange of communication and impressions is more or less constant. Very often the transfer of these impressions is made from the ego to the outer self during dreams or visions, while the outer self is partially asleep or on the so-called borderline of consciousness. At other times the transfer of impressions is made through the faculties of intuition, or a sort of urge within.

The important point to keep in mind is that we should not judge the degree or amount of contact communication thus being carried on by the degree or amount of knowledge which is transferred to the outer self; for only a small amount of such knowledge ever crosses the *borderline* and becomes known to the objective consciousness.

Of course, processes of development, concentration, meditation, and experiments will enable a man or woman to utilize the faculties that have been given him to bring about such transference of thought from the inner self to the outer self at will. This is one of the phases of mystical development known to the Orientals and to the members of the Rosicrucian brotherhood and similar bodies of mystics and metaphysicians throughout the world.

When the soul and ego are freed from the physical body, however, and return to the cosmic realm, the personality with its mind and memory remains as part of the soul; and direct communication with other egos, both on the cosmic plane and the earth plane is maintained with the same degree of accuracy and intimacy as before transition. This is true to such an extent that persons living on the earth plane and who are mystically developed, or who know the process of attuning the outer and inner selves for the purpose of transferring impressions, very often receive knowledge or impulses of thought which are difficult to classify, inasmuch as it is often impossible to tell whether the inner self has received these impressions or impulses from the ego of a person living on earth or an ego that is in the spiritual realm awaiting reincarnation.

In other words, messages or impressions may come to our inner selves, or to our psychic minds and egos, not only from the persons living around us on this earth plane, but from egos that are now dwelling on the cosmic plane in the interval between incarnations.

Nothing said in the foregoing paragraphs should be taken as an implied verification of the claims of the modern spiritualistic movement which contends that the soul or "spirit" of those who have passed on *returns to earth* and delivers messages to those who are still living here. Nothing in this chapter can be interpreted in that sense, for it is a fact that neither the soul nor the so-called spirit of a departed person *returns to earth* except to reincarnate in a physical body and remain here for a certain period of time. You will understand, therefore, that I am intimating that there is a different process and method whereby the divine mind or ego within us can communicate with the egos of those who have passed on, without manifesting any of the conventions and claims of the spiritualistic movement.

While these egos of departed personalities are existing on the cosmic plane they maintain the dominant nature of the last personality expressed on earth. I have shown in previous chapters that each personality is an aggregation of personalities, or, in other words, an accumulation of the essential elements of preceding personalities. And, after transition the ego of each individual maintains the same dominant personality that it had during its last incarnation in a physical body on earth. It is, however, always conscious of its preceding characterizations, although these are in the background, so to speak, and are like memories of our childhood.

Therefore, the man who was successively the farmer, the physician, the soldier, and then the banker, and who passed into the spiritual realm as a banker, would retain the dominant personality of a banker, while awaiting reincarnation, although he would be conscious of the fact that in the past he had also been farmer, physician, soldier, and perhaps many other characters in earthly lives. Even the name by which this personality was known in its last incarnation on earth is maintained as an identification symbol during the period of cosmic existence. It is not until the soul and ego enters into a new body for another incarnation on earth that the name of the last personality is laid aside and the dominant characteristics are placed in the background and new ones formed.

Thus we find in the spiritual realm millions of egos or personalities awaiting reincarnation. Some have been there for many years; some for only a few days or a few hours. Some will reincarnate tomorrow or the next day or years from now, all according to the cycles of life as explained in the preceding chapter. Some of these egos in the Cosmic at the present time have the personalities of infants, for their transition occurred early after birth or in childhood; others are the egos of youths; and others of old age. But all are equal in soul essence, in divine power, and wisdom, although *unequal* in world-experience and world-attainment.

It is in this cosmic realm that we find these egos dwelling in the *Mansions of the Soul.* These mansions are mentioned in many places in the Bible, and from what we can understand through these references, and by the impressions transmitted to us by the egos dwelling there, it would appear that the egos of all human beings are privileged to dwell in twelve divisions of the cosmic realm like unto twelve chambers in a great temple, and that each ego awaiting reincarnation enjoys the privilege of dwelling in one of these twelve mansions until it is time for reincarnation. These twelve mansions are mentioned or described in the nineteenth chapter of the book of Matthew, in the twenty-seventh to thirtieth verses, as twelve thrones, and elsewhere in the Holy Bible and the sacred writings of many peoples, these mansions are given various names and allegorical representations. Even Jesus mentioned them by saying that in his Father's house were many mansions, and he told his disciples that he was going to leave them to ascend to the heavenly realm to prepare a place for them.

In these *Mansions of the Soul* the personalities dwell in preparation for reincarnation and receive knowledge and divine benedictions which purge them of their errors for which they have made repentance, and which they have freely confessed. This bathes them with new effulgence so that they are more evolved and more highly developed for their new mission in life.

The sins committed by these personalities in the previous life on earth, and which constitute their karmic debts, are known to them while in the spiritual realm and, while they are forgiven for these sins, and they are purged of the blot upon their characters, they realize that they must return to earth and make compensation for each sin and each error and that only in this wise can such sins and errors be adjusted. Therefore, while these egos or personalities dwell in these mansions and are prepared to live more noble lives in the future, they are also prepared to return to earth and work out their salvation by compensating for their sins and living a life of adjustment.

During their regeneration in the *Mansions of the Soul* these egos become keenly aware of their previous mistakes, and the repentance and regret in their hearts and their burning desires to undo the wrongs they have done and make compensation constitute the factors and conditions which men have been pleased to call *hell* and *purgatory*. But the real suffering which each individual must endure for the suffering he has caused or the evil he has committed *is not suffering on the part of the soul,* but a *suffering of the flesh*, for it is the flesh that has committed the sin, and it is the flesh that must compensate through suffering. Therefore, the soul and ego must become incarnated again on earth in order to take on a body and be possessed of flesh which can suffer, and can compensate, and thereby make proper adjustment. The real *hell* of the flesh is therefore *on earth,* for the flesh cannot suffer *after transition,* and in the spiritual world there is no flesh to suffer.

These are the facts regarding the conditions and circumstances of the egos or personalities awaiting reincarnation as learned through cosmic contact, divine revelation, and the recollection of the ego's memory. Again the student of

sacred literature and the Holy Bible will find in these principles a further understanding of the allegorical statements
made in such writings and and explanation of many of the
parables and stories told by Jesus Christ to his disciples.

CHAPTER 15

MULTIPLE AND SECONDARY PERSONALITIES

A few years ago the public became acquainted with many new theories regarding the self, the ego, or the personality of human beings through the unique arguments introduced in public trials or in the newspaper discussions of the criminal acts of prominent persons. Such terms as *dementia americana* and *exaggerated ego* were the first to be made public and these were followed by a unique description of the "little man" who took possession of a sane and sensible person and caused him to commit murder. Later on more conservative psychologists or learned students of the human ego introduced the terms *multiple personalities* and *secondary personalities.*

All of these terms were used to imply that the average human being was a mixture of two or more personalities, one of which was the outer or general personality and the others deeply rooted in the inner self or inner consciousness.

The scientific experiments conducted by the eminent leaders of psychical research in England and America further developed the idea that whenever the outer or general personality of the average human being could be inhibited or made inactive, as in a trance or through deep concentration and relaxation, one or more of the *secondary personalities* or inner selves would take possession of the body and supplant the outer personality. The expression of the belief on the part of recognized scientists opened wide the doors to the unscientific minds in the spiritualistic field and they immediately seized upon these beliefs and the scientific terminology, and we heard much for many years about the secondary personalities of so-called mediums.

Fortunately, the continued research of scientists brought to light certain facts regarding human personalities and especially regarding the so-called secondary personalities, and these facts gradually robbed the whole subject of its mystery and prevented any further development of the superstitious or spiritualistic beliefs regarding such personalities in connection with showy demonstrations in questionable seance rooms. The subject of secondary personalities has at last been taken out of the speculative, superstitious, and magical fields of demonstration, and put into the truly scientific field of psychical research.

Many of the most wonderful examples of automatic writing or automatic dictation are unquestionably beautiful examples of the existence and functioning of a secondary personality, and how a secondary personality may control the functioning of the mind and of the hand in writing or speaking.

In such circumstances the secondary personality assumes a name for itself, presumably the name which it once legitimately possessed, and expresses itself with all of the characteristics with which that personality was presumably once very familiar and well known. It is not unusual, therefore, to find this secondary personality very different in many important essentials from the present general outer personality. In some cases there is a difference in sex, a difference in nationality or tongue, and a considerable difference in education, tastes, abilities, and desires.

In the case of those demonstrations where the secondary personality has been of value because of its unusual writings or dictations, it was found that the secondary personality had an education far superior to that of the outer personality. In some cases the secondary personality was learned in the arts and philosophy, possessed a high degree of literary and ethical culture, and expressed itself in beautiful thoughts truly worthy of publication. In some other cases, however, the secondary personality has been found to be illiterate and uncouth in its expressions and almost wholly the opposite of the outer personality.

The measure of genuineness of the secondary personality lies in its continued and consistent expression of a definite nature. With tests made over a long period of time it has been found that the writings of some of these secondary personalities are consistently of the same literary style, with no slips that reveal any forced or artificial tendency, and with an excellent recollection or memory of events and conditions, persons, and things associated with its life as an entity.

In other words, continued study of some of these secondary personalities has conclusively shown that so far as distinctiveness of character, distinctiveness of education and worldly experiences are concerned, the secondary personality is like unto a separate entity having lived at some time, somewhere, separated from the present outer personality.

To make this a little more understandable to those who have not been inclined to study the subject of secondary personalities we will use one illustration. For nearly fourteen years I was president of the New York Institute for Psychical Research. During that time the organization held monthly and semi-monthly meetings of a regular nature with many special sessions in between these, when unique investigations were necessary. I think that in those fourteen years our members investigated over one hundred cases of so-called secondary personalities or cases of automatic writing, automatic dictation, or automatic expression through the ouija board. Many of these cases were not worthy of more than one evening of test, for there was either evidence of wilful deception on the part of the outer personality or such a blending of the outer and the secondary personality that the two could not be separated in the writings and dictations. On the other hand, there were many genuine and intensely interesting cases which we watched for many years. I will take one of these as an illustration.

Mrs. J. B. was the wife of a prominent attorney in New York City. She had received an ordinary school education with one year at high school. She was of a fairly well-educated family of moderate circumstances and had received the usual instruction in the ordinary principles of ethics and culture. Her husband was a graduate of a university, but interested, however, in no other intellectual pursuit than his law studies. He prospered well during the first two years of his practice and then married, and during the two following years he accumulated sufficient funds to occupy a very fine home in New York and to provide his wife with many luxuries.

Mrs. J. B. was a very kind, loving, and sympathetic woman of about forty years of age, with a magnetic personality and a charming manner which made her an excellent hostess. During the course of their many social affairs at home it was discovered that Mrs. J. B. had developed a sympathetic attunement with her husband to such an extent that she was conscious of many of his strongest thoughts or emotions even when he was many miles absent from her. One incident of this will indicate what I mean.

On one occasion when the members of the society were all assembled at this lady's home, preparing for a test of her automatic writing, two of us suddenly and spontaneously thought of a test of her attunement with her husband. Mrs. J. B. at that moment was in the large reception room of her home with a group of the women members about her and was animatedly engaged in a discussion of frocks, and dresses, and other matters of this sort, while three or four of the men were with Mr. J. B. at the front door of his home under an awning, smoking and waiting for the meeting to be called to order.

Without any preparation or any long consideration of the test, my companion took a pin and suddenly jabbed it into the arm of Mr. J. B. as though by accident. Mr. J. B. jumped, and an expression of pain came into his face, but there was no outcry, for he was the type of man who would immediately control himself in any condition of pain or suffering of any kind. However, less than a fraction of a second after Mr. J. B. felt the pain there was a loud and uncanny outcry from Mrs. J. B. in the other part of the house, fully seventy-five feet distant from him and separated by several rooms filled with fifty or more persons talking and moving about.

The moment Mrs. J. B. cried out we rushed to her side, as did others, joining the group that was standing about her. She immediately said, "John has just had a pain in his arm, right here, and I felt it, and I want to see what happened to him." She indicated correctly where the pain was caused by the pin, and in joining him she stated that she felt the pain at the same time that he did. She said it was a common thing for her to feel any sharp pain which he felt.

It was not her attunement with Mr. J. B. that interested us, however, but her automatic writing. For hours she would sit at a table with pencil and sheets of paper before her and write thousands of words of philosophy, advice, comments, or incidents of the past, descriptions of persons and principles, etc., without hesitancy or without seeming to become tired. Before beginning her writing she would sit in a relaxed position with pencil in her hand resting on the sheets of paper and wait for some gradual change that came over her inwardly or outwardly, and when this change was completed the hand holding the pencil would suddenly begin to write extremely rapidly, and Mrs. J. B. would often close her eyes and keep them closed for a half-hour at a time while sheet after sheet of paper was filled more rapidly than the average human can write coherently and profoundly.

In answer to questions, which were always reluctantly answered, this personality that expressed itself in the automatic writing claimed to be the "inner" self of Mrs. J. B., and claimed that the personality of Mrs. J. B. with which we were familiar was only an infant personality that was trying to usurp the position of the *real self* within. This "real self" gave us the name of *Clara W.* It refused, however, to tell where it had ever lived or when. Its writings, however, revealed much in this regard.

It showed very intimate acquaintance with many sections of the New England states and with towns and rivers in certain sections which were very old. It referred to buildings and especially to several churches which had existed in those towns a hundred years previous, but were now either in ruins or completely gone. It also referred to persons living in those citites who were no longer living. It was thoroughly familiar with music and the harmonics of music, although Mrs. J. B. herself could play no musical instrument and had never been known, even among most intimate friends, to have anything more than a casual interest in music. This secondary personality was also well read in certain lines of literature of a profoundly Puritanical nature and likewise familiar with the Bible, and with certain religious beliefs that clearly classified its religious denomination.

In the philosophical writings the expressions were always Puritanical, somewhat narrow, but nevertheless kind and sympathetic. In all of the years that Mrs. J. B. wrote there was never an expression or even a word that was not absolutely consistent with all that had been written and expressed by this personality in previous writings, and even though the same questions were asked many years apart, the answers were always the same as proved by comparison of the writings. Mrs. J. B. never had any copies of the writings to retain and, therefore, could not have prepared herself for the future questions.

This separate personality of hers was unquestionably a distinct entity at some previous time, and today it was an imprisoned secondary personality striving at times to regain its control of her physical body. I mentioned her close attunement with her husband only because it was this unusual fact that first made both the man and his wife realize that her mentality or spirituality was of a nature slightly different from the average human being, and it led them into investigating the laws and principles of human personality. Whether Mrs. J. B. had any other unusual psychic development or not I cannot say at this time, for our research work was limited to a study of her secondary personality.

Now, Mrs. J. B is no different from millions of other men and women. Back of this secondary personality in Mrs. J. B. was another personality, and back of that one still another, etc. Many tests conducted in Europe and America have revealed that the existence of three and four personalities of a distinct nature. These *multiple personalities* are unquestionably the result of previous incarnations, as explained in previous chapters of this book. The interesting point, however, is that the study of secondary personalities has become quite systematized and has been reduced to a very definite field.

The investigators of secondary personalities are not interested in any doctrines or principles involving the reason for the existence of such personalities, or how or when they came into the human being. They are interested only in the present manifestation of such personalities. Such research and study has brought to light many interesting facts. Primarily, it has revealed that each one of us is at times influenced by the rising demands, desires, urges, or inclinations of a secondary personality that seems to be just across the border from our outer personality. In other words, so far as personalities are concerned, there seem to be two in each human body trying to have dominance over the objective faculties and functioning. When the secondary personality is inclined to differ in taste, desires, and ways of living with those of the present outer personality, there is sure to be some conflict, and this conflict will express itself in the form of contrary or strange complexities which beset the even tenor of our lives.

Often the desire to travel or to visit certain foreign lands, or to indulge in certain habits or practices, or to taste of certain foods, is the result of an uprising unconsciousness of the submerged personality. A pious and good person may be tempted to evil deeds in this way, and an evil person may be tempted to good deeds through the inclinations or urges of a secondary personality. This secondary personality may also manifest itself in periods of dreams or meditation, when the outer self is partially dormant and relaxed. Certain diseased conditions or injuries may bring on prolonged periods of dormancy to the outer self and permit the secondary personality to take entire control of the mind and faculties of the body. In such cases the person would manifest different traits, habits, customs of living, and mannerisms of speech, and would seem to be an entirely different person.

There are only two possible explanations for the existence of secondary or multiple personalities. One is the belief that someone outside, or the personality of a person now living, or who has passed into the Beyond, has temporarily *possessed* our bodies and submerged our outer personality and supplanted it with its own. In other words, being "possessed" is one explanation. Such an explanation, however, resorts to what may be called *supernatural laws and prin-*

ciples, or *supernatural beliefs*, and it resembles too greatly the ancient superstitions and beliefs in the existence of *evil entities* which can take possession of us and control us. The only other explanation for secondary or multiple personalities is that they are *the remnants of our own previous existences on earth.* Such an explanation does not resort to supernatural principles or to any unique or irrational principle in life.

Of the two explanations you have your choice. If you discard the doctrine of reincarnation and refuse to believe that we have ever lived before on this earth plane, or ever had any other personality of our own than the one that is generally known as our present outer personality, then you must believe that the great mass of scientific evidence showing the existence of multiple personalities and the easy manifestation of a secondary personality is proof that the human consciousness can be possessed or submerged by another personality and enslaved by it for a short or long period. Certainly it is more difficult for the sane and rational mind to believe that God in creating us and in putting his own divine consciousness within us also permitted of our enslavement by other personalities, than it is to believe in the rational doctrines of reincarnation.

CHAPTER 16

SOULS OF ANIMALS AND
"THE UNBORN"

The question often arises as to whether animals lower in species than the human being have souls and what becomes of these souls after transition. Again this question occasionally implies that each animal has a distinct and separate soul which is in nowise connected with any other soul of the universe.

We cannot know of the so-called animal soul what we have been able to learn regarding the human soul for obvious reasons, but we do know that there is an Oversoul essence for all of the animal kingdom as there is for the human beings of the universe. This universal soul essence pervades the bodies of every living thing in the animal kingdom. Incidentally we may add that there is also a universal soul essence for every living thing in the vegetable and mineral kingdoms.

Unquestionably, the personality or character element of the animal soul passes through stages of evolution and development like that of the human. I mean by this that the soul character of a dog, for instance, will evolve and progress through various incarnations until it becomes a well-trained, well-educated, and highly intellectual character or personality. In other words, the soul personality of a fox terrier will reincarnate in the bodies of fox terriers from time to time and in this way evolve to a very intellectual character. The soul character of a fox terrier will continue to incarnate in the bodies of fox terriers until it has attained a certain degree of perfection and then will start a new cycle of incarnations in a larger or more highly developed animal body.

Judging the cycle from this point of view we would say that the soul personalities and characters of the animal kingdom pass through various incarnations in each species and then start a new cycle in the next higher or next progressive stage of animal development. A study of the intellect of animals on the part of specialists has revealed that there is a progressive stage of intellect in the animal kingdom. By some of these experts the horse is considered the most highly developed from an intellectual point of view; by others the dog is considered the most highly developed. The elephant also runs high in this line of progression. No attempt has ever been made to classify properly the various species of animals from such a point of view and the subject has not attracted the attention and serious study that it really warrants.

Theoretically it may be true that the animal soul begins its first cycle of earthly incarnations in the lowest or smallest or most inconsequential species. The size of the animal cannot be one of the factors in determining the intellectual progress; it is known, for instance, that among the insects the bee and ant show almost the same degree of evolved intelligence, although there is a great difference in the size of their bodies. There are many animals much smaller than the largest snakes which show an intelligence superior to the snakes, and an ability to outwit them in any contest of intellect. The rhinoceros with its huge body does not begin to have the intellect of many small animals.

Association with human beings is unquestionably one of the factors that enters into the progressive development of the character and personality of the soul of animals. Whether this special development of intellect on the part of such animals is due to special objective training which they have received at the hands of humans, or whether Nature has especially decreed that certain animals shall be more highly developed intellectually in order to serve man more efficiently, is a matter that remains to be determined through careful study.

For instance, those who have been devoting their time to this study for some years have not yet reached a conclusion as to whether in India and other lands the association of the elephant with humans, who have trained him to do very efficient work and render unusual service, has resulted in the development of a high degree of intellect in the elephant or whether the cosmic conception of the soul personality in the elephant was originally decreed to be of a high stage in order that the elephant might serve man in many ways. The latter assumption seems to be the most universal opinion, and it will not minimize the effect that man's training has had upon the elephant's intelligence. It may truly be that the elephant was preordained to serve man as he does and is born with a high degree of intelligence in order to fulfill his special services and this higher intelligence has been added to and strengthened by training and association with human beings.

In regard to the structural anatomy and special physiological characteristics of certain animals, we know that they have been cosmically prepared and uniquely evolved to fill certain places in the scheme of things and to contend with certain conditions. The camel, for instance, is most uniquely qualified to contend with life upon desert land where water is scarce, and to battle against sandstorms and other conditions of life in the desert. Whether the animal has gradually evolved to such qualifications in a physiological sense or was originally created with them is outside of our present scope of study. Undoubtedly the continued struggle with certain conditions in desert life has tended to evolve in each successive generation of the camel a more efficiently equipped creature better prepared to meet such conditions. If this is true in the physiological sense it most certainly would be true in the intellectual, mental, or character sense.

The idea, however, that the soul personality of an animal, lower in development than that of the human being, can eventually evolve into a degree of perfection where it is prepared to enter the body of a human being as a sort of *primitive human soul personality* is an idea that had its origin in ancient beliefs and is not supported by any actual facts found by those who have spent their lifetimes in investigating the subject.

It is probably true that the physical body of man in its anatomical and physiological sense has passed through many stages of *material evolution.* There is no question about the fact that the earliest forms of primitive man were crude and far more homely and lacking in certain refinements than the human form of today. There is every possible evidence to prove that man's physical form has grown in gradual stages from a more beast-like appearance to the present refined appearance. Despite the fact, however, that we can take the physical form of man and trace its development backwards to periods when the human arms were longer, or the feet larger, or the head and brain capacity less developed, with nostrils larger, the ears bigger, and the muscles stronger, there is no reason for the belief that we can ever continue this line of development backward to a point where the human form was no longer human, *but entirely beastly*. In other words, the fact that man in his primitive form was more or less animal-like does not warrant the belief that there were stages of development before this in which man was either of the monkey, gorilla, or any other animal species.

Man as a *distinct species* was created at the same time that all the other animal species were created. Regardless of the fact that in some period of man's development his body was far more beastly than it is now, he was at that time so far superior to any other species of the animal kingdom that he was unquestionably the highest type of animal creation and had certain faculties and physiological attributes as well as soul character that made him the essential *image of God*, and far above any other creature.

Man's environment and his mode of living have had some effect upon the physiological changes that have taken place in his body, but his evolving mentality and soul character, from one incarnation to another, are responsible for the changes in his environment and for the improvements that he has made. The soul personality of man has ever struggled to reach greater heights of development and perfection, and has always held before it the ideal of cosmic attunement and eventual oneness with God. This in itself would lift man gradually into a better environment which he would create for himself, and while these improved environments have had their reaction upon his physical condition, it is a fact that man has made his environment rather than the environment has made man.

The wearing of shoes has had a considerable effect upon the formation of human feet and is bound to have a still greater effect in future centuries, for the physical body will gradually adjust itself to enforced physical conditions; but after all it is man who created the shoes and who is responsible, therefore, for the effect that shoes have had upon him. The same can be said of many other things in the life of man. The greatest effect upon man's physical being, however, has been the result of the development of the intellect and of the soul personality within.

What becomes of the soul character in the most highly developed animals is something that we cannot answer. Elimination of the belief that a highly developed animal soul personality can some day enter into the body of a savage man and begin its career as a human personality leaves us without any explanation or understanding of the future or ultimate purpose of the animal soul personality.

Sentiment, of course, has tended to make many believe that the soul of a pet animal, especially a highly intelligent dog which has manifested many traits of character in understanding human thought, may some day become the *primitive soul essence* of a human being. It is not an unkind or irreverential idea but wholly one that is unsupported by any evidence.

Let us take, for instance, the highly intelligent dog which accompanied Commander Byrd on his expedition to the South Pole. This dog, which had always been the leader of the group of other dogs that led the first sleigh into all of the unknown regions of Byrd's previous expeditions, revealed a high degree of intellect, human understanding, and intuition. When the dog became injured, and yet insisted upon facing the storms of the South Pole and appeared broken-hearted when he could not lead the expedition sleigh, it was found necessary to shoot him and bury his body in the ice of that barren part of the world in order that he would not starve or freeze to death, causing suffering which none of the men could bear to think about.

What is to become of this highly evolved dog character and personality? The men who loved that dog would like to think or believe that some day it will be born again and reach a higher state of development. This is possible, but nothing can warrant our belief that the development of this soul character will take place in the body of a human being, of even a most primitive form of development.

Everything that we know of the human soul indicates that it is a part of the divine Oversoul of the universe, which is the consciousness and divine essence of God; and that this consciousness and creative essence was established in the universe by God, who resides in the image of his own likeness as a definite species of the animal kingdom called *man*. This divine Oversoul, which provides the human soul characters and personalities throughout the universe, must always exist intact, since God created mankind and has never added to or subtracted from it through any of the evolved processes that are taking place in the lower manifestations of nature.

The next interesting point in connection with the human soul is in regard to those soul characters or personalities which were destined to enter human bodies at birth, but were unable to do so because of an interference with the life of the body. The question is often asked as to what takes place when a human body is born lifeless or it fails to reach its full degree of embryonic development.

It must be noted that a human soul character, or personality, does not begin to function in a human body until the first breath of life is breathed into the nostrils. The soul that is to enter an unborn body is known to hover over the expectant mother and to envelop both the mother and unborn child for some time preceding birth; and unquestionably some of the soul essence permeates every part of the mother and unborn child; but there is no functioning of this soul in the body of the little child until the child begins to breathe and is a *distinct entity* in a physiological and psychological sense. Throughout all of the mystical sacred writings of the past we find the thought that is expressed in the book of Genesis stated plainly and positively. The body of man is formed out of dust or elements of the earth, but does not become a living soul until the breath of life is breathed into its nostrils or taken into its body and it becomes living in consciousness and all of its functionings.

A soul, therefore, drawn from the Cosmic toward an unborn child envelops both the mother and body of the child awaiting birth. If the little body is born lifeless or fails to breathe, if it is prematurely born lifeless or is destroyed or injured in the early stages of its embryonic development, the soul fails to enter the body in a functional sense. As soon as the little body is separated from the mother and is no longer vitalized but wholly lifeless, the waiting soul personality with its vital essence returns to the Cosmic from whence it came and there is no incarnation or earthly existence in the little body.

What effect this may have upon the soul character is not known and it is mere speculation to express even an opinion. If the little newborn body takes but a few breaths, or the organs are conscious of the bodily functions for a short time, even though that be but an hour or two, the soul has entered the little body and has started its earthly career. If transition follows thereafter, it is similar to the transition that occurs at any time during the earthly life of any individual. This is all that can be said on this subject with positive knowledge.

The belief that any destruction or injury to the embryonic body of the unborn child is an injury to the soul is merely a sentimental thought with a rightful reverential attitude of mind. Unquestionably the destruction of the human body or embryo in any stage of its existence from conception to maturity is a sin, since it is a sin against the process of nature and, therefore, a sin against the plans of God. But it is a mistaken idea to believe that any destruction or injury can have any effect upon the soul of the child, for even after its birth no accident or injury to the body of a human being can injure or harm the divine, immortal essence and consciousness of the soul.

CHAPTER 17

RECOLLECTIONS OF THE PAST

O ne of the arguments most often used in an attempt to deny the possibility of reincarnation is this: If we have lived once before and our memory retains any knowledge of that existence, why is it that we do not recall any event of our previous lives?

You will note that this question, no matter how it may be worded, always includes the positive statement or the positive intimation that no one ever recalls anything of his previous incarnations. The question is really not a question but a statement and precludes any argument, since it assumes right from the very start that no one does recall anything of the past.

Such an attitude is absolutely unfair for two reasons. In the first place, no one has a right to assume because he or she has no distinct recollection of a previous existence that no one else has; and, second, it is not right to assume that the mind does not occasionally reveal to us real pictures of the past which we do not understand or appreciate as having any connection with the past.

To illustrate my point, I will refer to just one very recent and fortunate conversation. A businessman of conservative and orthodox religious viewpoints, wholly out of sympathy with the doctrine of reincarnation, called upon me in regard to my plans for a trip to Egypt and Palestine with a number of my co-workers. He frankly admitted that while he was not interested in the researches we intended to make or any of the ceremonies that we would attend while in Egypt, he nevertheless had a deep-rooted desire to go to these foreign lands but had never wanted to go alone. Now that a few persons in his city, whom he knew fairly well, were going with us, he wished to go along with them and enjoy their companionship on such a trip. Knowing from previous remarks made by him that he was out of sympathy with many of the thoughts expressed in this book, I asked him bluntly why he wanted to go to Egypt and Palestine rather than on any other tour. His first answer was this: "Because I have always felt a strange fascination or a peculiar attraction toward some part of Egypt or the Holy Land."

I tried to analyze his statement and find out what part of Egypt, or what things in Egypt and the Holy Land were responsible for the attraction he felt. His answers were always indefinite and vague until I finally drew from him the following: "Well, ever since I was a young man, I have felt that certain pictures I have seen of Egypt or Palestine were more interesting to me than pictures of any other part of the world. I do not mean pictures of the busy streets of Cairo, but of some of the outlying, native villages. I have always felt that I would find something there or discover something in such a locality that would be of intense interest and perhaps personal profit to me in some way."

Upon further investigation, he reluctantly admitted that some of the scenes he had seen of native villages and people with native costumes seemed "somewhat" familiar to him, and he further admitted that this fact had led him to read many different books on the history and customs of Egypt and the Holy Land. And, that in some passages describing incidents of a few centuries ago, he seemed to feel a familiarity, or a *sympathetic understanding,* as he put it, which only increased his attraction toward those countries.

I could not help smiling when he made these admissions with such reluctance, for I knew at once precisely what he was experiencing, and I also knew that it was useless at the present time to point out to him why certain incidents in history relating to certain localities and peoples and certain scenes and places connected therewith were "somewhat" familiar to him. I know that if I had pressed my questioning far enough, he would have admitted that some of these scenes were as familiar to him as though they had been seen by him sometime in a dream. This would have aroused his suspicion, however, and caused him to feel that I was trapping him into admissions which he did not care to make, and so I dropped the argument.

This experience on the part of this man is typical of that which can be found in the life of the average human being. I believe that in my lifetime I have questioned perhaps ten thousand people in regard to so-called recollections of the past. I have not called these things by that term, but have asked them frankly this question: "Do you ever find in your moments of meditation, contemplation, or revery, certain scenes of places, people, buildings, or homes, rising in your mind like pictures or scenes that were familiar to you?"

If this question is asked before anything is said about the subject of reincarnation, the average person one meets in the average walks of life will frankly admit that such is true in his case and that he has often wondered about it, and has really been puzzled about it. If the person to whom the question is put is one who has traveled much, especially in foreign lands, he will generally add that, "When I was traveling here or there, I was surprised suddenly to come upon a scene in front of a building (park, public square, bridge, or other picturesque setting) that I found to be precisely a duplicate of what I had seen in my mind many times, but which I had never before seen in real life."

When these persons say that they have come upon scenes which they had never seen before in real life, they always mean that they had never seen them in *this life* or in *this incarnation,* and they will frankly tell you that it was the first time that they had ever traveled or had been anywhere near the familiar scenes in their present earthly existence. If, then, you open the subject of reincarnation and ask them if it is not possible that the familiarity with such scenes may be due to having lived near them in a previous incarnation, you find some who are broad enough in their thinking to realize the possibility of this and admit that it may be true, whereas others will instantly tell you that since they do not *believe* in reincarnation, they cannot look upon these things as an indication of having lived once before.

This means that we must allow such persons to offer another theoretical explanation of why and how they have scenes coming before their consciousness with a certain degree of familiarity but which they have never seen in actuality. The explanations thus offered are often amusing and, of course, associated with extreme supernatural principles or impossible mental laws. In other words, the explanations do not explain at all. And yet these persons will seriously assure you that they do not have any recollections of a previous existence and, therefore, they certainly could not have lived at some other time.

On the other hand, nearly every person who has read of historical events in other lands at other times than at present has found himself strangely attuned with the history of certain periods or of certain places, and is attracted more to the history of these places than to other places Sometimes this interest is in relation to places in America or even in the same state where the person now lives, or often the places are located a few hundreds, a few thousand, or many thousands of miles away.

Then there are many human beings who in moments of reflection, relaxation, or revery find themselves slipping backward, so to speak, to a rapid panorama of scenes and incidents which seem to struggle to come up out of the fog and mist of past recollections, but cannot quite reveal themselves in all of the clearness and distinction that makes for perfect recognition. Persons who have experienced this are often puzzled, not only by the peculiar pictures that do come close to the borderline of clear perception, but by the multiplicity of scenes that seem to flash so rapidly in the background of the consciousness. There are also many who have had certain definite impressions come to them from the depths of their consciousness, which seem to be related to their own lives in a time and period long past. These persons, too, are puzzled over these things, but seldom associate them with anything like a past existence.

Now, just what should one expect in regard to the recollection of events in a past life? Is it logical for the average human being to expect that the events of a past life should be registered in a memory so close to the borderline of our present consciousness that we can easily reach across or pierce through the veil that separates the past from the present and bring these pictures into living reality? Assuming that the memory we have now is the same memory that we have had in a previous life, and assuming that in its storehouse vaults it retains all of the pictures and impressions registered upon it throughout all of our lives, is it logical to suppose that it should be an easy and simple thing to reach into those vaults and unlock the records *at will* and withdraw clear and distinct pictures relating to any period of time? If you believe that this is logical, then it is reasonable for me to ask why it is not possible for you to reach right into your storehouse of memory now and withdraw all the scenes, all the pictures, relating to the events of your life in the present incarnation during your life in the present incarnation during your second, third, and fourth years of childhood. Can you do this?

You may answer and tell me that you do recall certain incidents of your childhood and youth very distinctly. At best, you may tell me of ten incidents clearly registered in your mind and easily recalled, which relate to your earliest years. But, think of the millions of other impressions and pictures that are locked in that memory and which you cannot recall. The few that you speak of constitute such a small fraction, and such a small fragment, that it is hardly worth speaking about as an illustration of recollection.

Let us examine the few that you do recall, and let us see how clear and distinct they are. Do you remember the first time you were allowed to play on the street or to play with your neighborhood companions? You may answer by picking out one incident connected with this important event in your life. But, if we analyze that incident, we find, first of all, that there is some unusual feature connected with it, which not only impressed you very profoundly at the time, but impressed your parents or your relatives, or your companions, and caused them to speak about it often. The event may have occurred in your second year, or your fourth year, but you will find that it was an event that was probably discussed and spoken about in your household for several years thereafter, and was not only registered in your mind and memory a number of times, but through repetition of description and the telling about it, it was carried along into your fifth or sixth year of life.

Then perhaps many times during your eighth or ninth year, you easily recalled that event and spoke about it, and heard others speak about it, and so it was once again brought up out of the musty old records of the past into the present and was again registered in your eighth or ninth year, even though it had originally occurred in the second, third, or fourth year. Now, perhaps during your twelfth year, it was recalled again by some similar event or some family discussion, and once more the picture and incident that was becoming slightly vague and preparing to fade into the indefiniteness of the past was revived and recolored and strengthened in its details and registered once more in your twelfth year.

This may have happened so many times in your life that this particular incident out of millions of others has been refreshed from time to time and brought from the *past* into the *now,* until when you want to recall it *now*, you only have to reach back to the last time that you registered the incident to revive it, and bring it into close examination.

You will admit that such an incident is not typical of all the incidents of your past. To prove this, you can take any one of the incidents of your childhood, which you easily recall, and after having described it and painted it in all of its fullness of reality, ask yourself this question: What did I do the next day after this incident, or what did I do that same afternoon or evening? Certainly, if you reach into your past easily and quickly and get in contact with a certain day or hour of your past life as a child, you should be able to move the finger of recollection along the unwritten records to the next few lines and recall what happened a few hours after the incident you relate. Can you do that?

Usually, the few incidents of childhood that are easily recalled are not only those which have been revived from time to time, as stated above, but they are widely separated from each other in nature and in period of time, and the great gaps in between these events remain absolutely unrecalled. Does this not tend to prove that although a perfect record of all events in the past is retained in the mind, the matter of recollection is not so easy, and it is not given to man to have free access to all of these impressions?

If you ask why it is that it is not as easy to recall all of the events of a certain day or month twenty-five years ago as it is to recall the events of yesterday or last week, let me point out to you the psychological fact that our present consciousness of ourselves is always in the nature of a central point in a large picture, and this picture contains the events of the last few days. As we go backward, past the few recent days, the picture extends itself into vagueness and indefiniteness. Today we are conscious not only of ourselves and our immediate surroundings, but we are conscious of the things we did this morning and of the plans we made for this afternoon, tonight, and tomorrow. We are right now in the center of a whirling mass of impressions and this gives us consciousness of ourselves and our relationship to persons and places. But man would soon lose saneness and soundness of mind and become a hopeless maniac if there were in the borderline of his present consciousness the living, vibrating impressions of all the things that had occurred in his past life or since childhood.

As each day passes, the pictures and impressions that were alive and active in the consciousness for a while are slowly taken from it and placed away in the records of the memory. It is like the librarian in a large library who makes it his business each morning when he finds new copies of new issues of magazines and periodicals on his desk to go into the reading room of the library and deposit these new issues and collect those which are becoming old and place them away in the reference files to be called for on demand. If the old ones were allowed to accumulate while the new ones were constantly added, there would soon be such a litter of publications on the reading table as to make it impossible to be aware of which were new and which were old.

So we find that while the records of the past are stored away indelibly, they can only be recalled by association of ideas or by some special process which enables us to pick one impression or one scene at at time from the past records and bring it into the now. Sometimes, through the association of ideas or the similarity of scenes and events, a picture or impression of the past is brought into present realization. The older that impression is, or the more ancient the picture, the more vague and indefinite it is, until some of these are like fantastic sketches on a transparent surface through which we can see so clearly as to make the picture almost invisible. If this is true regarding events which have occurred within our present lives and which are not more than 30, 40, or 50 years of age, think of how indefinite must be the impressions stored away in the memory and which are 100 or 200 years old.

According to the cycles of reincarnation, the average man or woman of today would have ended the last previous incarnation on earth about 100 to 130 years ago. That means that one would have to reach back at least 130 years in order to have impressions of the last years of that previous existence. If 30 or 40 years will soften pictures and impressions and cover them with a mystic veil of indefiniteness, 100 years would surely make them very vague and very faint, indeed. Only the most impressive, the most psychological, and important of such ancient pictures and impressions, perhaps written and printed in blood or pain, suffering, trial, and anxiety, would be so indelibly impressed as to retain brilliancy at the present time.

Is it any wonder, then, that in our reveries and meditation, we have but faint pictures and impressions coming to us like familiar scenes, and these are never frivolous things or connected with mere transitory conditions. Impressions of a city or of a building, or of a race of people, of a park, or a bridge, or something of this kind may be the registered pictures that accumulated in the memory through years of serious contact with them and are, therefore, more indelibly impressed than the mere passing events of one day or one hour.

However, there are those human beings who have at times found many definite recollections in connection with certain events that were of more than ordinary importance in their past lives. On one of my trips through Europe a companion traveler seeking for a certain castle that he had seen in pictures and which seemed familiar, suddenly came upon it when he did not expect to do so. It was late in the evening and by artificial light he saw only the remnants of an old iron gateway in a huge wall. This had been no part of the picture he had in his mind. But, as he stood before it with me, wondering where the gateway led to, he suddenly recalled or felt a degree of familiarity with that opening in the wall. Turning to me, he said: "If there is another small doorway inside of the enclosure of this wall whereby a person can walk down a few steps and pass under the wall, then I know where I am."

With our flashlights and lantern, we went inside the old and abandoned enclosure and found, fifty feet away, another opening in the wall closed with remnants of wood and much shrubbery, and which led down twelve steps to a tunnel under the wall. And this in turn led to an underground chamber which my companion perfectly described to me before we entered it. Returning again to the highway and our hotel, we waited until daybreak and then found in the center of this walled enclosure the old building that he had described to me so often in our interviews in America, and for which he had been searching in Europe. The interior of this great building was precisely as he had described it. In fact, we had some trouble in having a doorway opened to another underground passageway and chamber, which my companion described accurately before we entered it, and which the guide and authorities of the village claimed had not been opened for one hundred years or more because of its dangerous condition and the difficulty in reaching it.

My companion claimed that he had either lived or labored in and around this place, and that his duties took him especially into these underground places, which were probably wine cellars in his time. I cite this illustration to show that one picture, one impression, one thought, may associate itself with another and serve as a key to unlock a number of related pictures and impressions. The sight of that old gate in the wall recalled to this man's mind the fact that there was another archway in the wall leading to an underground room. This he had never recalled in all of his other talks about a castle and its many rooms. Very often, the sight of one part of a building or part of a city will instantly recall from memory other related pictures and impressions which seem so familiar to us that we feel we could write about them, paint them, and reach out and touch them.

Whence come these impressions, these pictures?—not from our present lifetime experience, surely, for most of these things relate to distant and faraway places which we have not contacted in the present life.

Then, we have the cases that are quite frequent where a child or an adult suffering under some unusual mental or psychological condition is placed in a state where the storehouse of the memory suddenly unlocks itself and reveals a mass of its impressions and pictures in living brilliancy and without restraint. One case of this kind was that of a young girl in a hospital in Montreal, who could speak only French and knew nothing of any foreign languages and was not well educated. This child was in the hospital for an operation against which she protested and fought with all the strength in her little body. Finally, as the last moments approached and the doctors were ready to take her into the operating room, she made one more struggle to battle with them. In her wild fury and frenzy, she threw herself into a hysterical state in which she screamed and laughed and wept. Unable to control her, they were about to strap her to a chair, when her fury again burst forth in the wildest talk that the doctors and nurses had ever heard.

This time the girl talked perfect English and told them that she had had this operation performed in a previous life, when she was thirty-five years of age, and had suffered so much from it that she refused to have it done again. She gave her name, her family name, the name of the town in which she had lived, and many other incidents of her life, and then suddenly relapsed again into quietness and could not remember later what she had said or that she had expressed such ideas. The use of perfect English and the strangeness of the facts she related induced the authorities to make an investigation and this was continued by several organizations and newspaper men. It was found in the town where she claimed to have lived and passed away that a woman of her age and name had lived there some eighty years previously and had passed away, and even the grave and tombstone were located, verifying the name and the date.

Only recently, in India, a young girl through illness entered into a peculiar psychic state in which she claimed that she recalled her previous life and knew where her previous relatives could be located. Eminent investigators accompanied the young child to the city she mentioned and which she had never seen in her present life. She led the investigators along a certain road previously described, to a certain building which she had also previously described, and there, beneath the flooring of one of the rooms, in a condition and position as she had predicted, they found an old box containing records which were identical with those that she had mentioned to them. These records proved the identity of the girl and verified her story.

Hundreds of such incidents as these have been recorded in the past and verified by every investigator who has looked into the matter. A complete list of these cases would make interesting reading, but would make a book of this kind too cumbersome. A denial of these facts is merely a denial of published knowledge beyond dispute.

Each one of us has in his memory, in the closed and sealed books of the past, a complete record of his previous experiences, impressions, and activities. These serve us at times as lessons learned and experiences to be used as standards to guide us in our present living. But because we cannot easily recall them, and cannot drag them out into the open as we would bring forth the things of yesterday, is no proof that they are not there, for when occasion requires, or when they will serve some purpose, they are available; and every person who has had considerable experience in the practice of certain psychological, metaphysical, and mystical laws has brought forth sufficient impressions from the past to prove at least one or two of his many past incarnations.

CHAPTER 18

THE FEAR OF DEATH

Perhaps one of the most beautiful and satisfying results of understanding the doctrines of reincarnation is the complete removal from our consciousness of any fear of so-called death.

I have known in my lifetime very intimately and among my closest kin, those who have suffered intensely in the latter part of their lives through this unexpressed though potent fear of inevitable transition. Among these were several who were unquestionably sincere and devoted Christians, and who found their only happiness in the contemplation of transition through believing that living the Christian life would save them from the torments of hell. But they found no happiness or joy in the prospect of a long period of unconscious existence in an unknown ethereal realm awaiting an ultimate Judgment Day.

The average Christian believes that at the time of transition his soul enters unknown realms to pass through unknown experiences, and then dwells in oblivion for an eternal length of time awaiting a Judgment Day before the rewards of goodness or right living can be enjoyed. He shudders, however, at the thought of this eternal sleep and loss of consciousness. You may say what you please, and sing the songs of your church rejoicing in the fact that after you have been found good and worthy you will dwell in the Spirit of God; but the fact remains that in the privacy of your own thoughts you are like millions of others who do not find the prospect of any happiness or pleasure in waiting for some Judgment Day so far distant that a seemingly endless period of time must be spent in total unconsciousness and oblivion.

Two factors enter into the cause of the usual fear of transition, as found in the hearts and minds of the average persons of the Western world. The first is the belief that socalled death may come upon them suddenly and cut short their careers, ambitions, and desires for achievement, and deprive them of their success in life. The businessman who has just entered into the working out of his life's ambitions, and is now venturing upon the realization of all of his hopes and plans, realizing that time is required to see the fulfillment of all that he has created, is always depressed and made unhappy by the thought of the grim figure of death stepping up to him and ending it all for all time. The young man or young woman just entering into the fullness of life and beginning to sense some happiness as a reward for all of the past waiting, hoping, praying, and suffering, fears death may come at any time and end it all.

Is there anything of a hopeful nature which these persons can find in a Western world orthodoxy? All that they can learn is that after the sudden closing of this life, they will be plunged into a place of purging for the cleansing of their sinful bodies and minds—or, if this does not happen, they will go into an eternal, unconscious sleep that is more dark and more void than anything known in this life, and they will remain in this state for an endless length of time, perhaps millions and billions of years, and then suddenly be brought before the Great Judge and either given eternal rewards or condemned to a place of punishment and purging.

Is there anything cheerful about this aspect, or this picture, of the future? Is there anything cheerful in the idea that at the end of this life, when transition comes, we are going to be held accountable for the sins we have inherited from Adam and Eve and our forebears, and for the sins that we have committed in ignorance and through lack of understanding, and that we shall suffer for these things without being given any opportunity to undo the wrongs, wipe away the sins, and live a life of goodness?

If our transition means the end of all of our earthly existence and that what we are at the time of that transition constitutes the picture or the record by which we are to be eternally judged, then transition is the beginning of a period of suffering, sorrow, and regret. Our inner nature cries aloud at the injustice of this. Even man's poorly invented and imperfectly conceived laws are more fair than this, for no man is held accountable for the sins of others, and his inability to know the laws and redeem himself is given consideration.

An understanding of the doctrines of reincarnation changes the entire viewpoint of life. First of all, it enables us to realize that the greatest sins which we have inherited are those which we have committed ourselves and for which we alone are responsible. Furthermore, it enables us to understand that the sins which we commit here and now through ignorance or lack of understanding may be compensated for and the slate wiped clean and a new start given, whereby we may live a joyful life and try once more to make the goal with a clean record. It helps us to understand the purposes of life and to find the benefits that lie in all of our trials and tribulations. We can understand why there may be a profitable lesson in the suffering we bring upon ourselves, if we are to have another opportunity to live again and through conscious memory of the present mistakes avoid them in the future. We can look forward to the time of inevitable transition without fear and even with hope if we know that it is not the end of all of our experiences, but merely the stopping of one journey and the beginning of another.

Through an understanding of the doctrines of reincarnation we are prepared to go ahead and create and build and evolve our plans and start them into action, realizing that if whatever we are doing is the real mission of our life, we should put all of our effort into it and do it well without any fear that our mission may be cut short and our desires unfulfilled. If transition comes before we have completed the great work we have started here, we know that if it is truly our great mission in life, we will come back and take it up again and carry it on to a grand fulfillment.

The doctrines of reincarnation teach us that so-called death is not the beginning of self-annihilation, or of a long and endless sleep, or of an eternal period of oblivion, but merely a change of earthly consciousness which will in nowise affect the inner consciousness or the consciousness of self, and that instead of a long dark sleep we shall be alive and among the living in the cosmic realm improving ourselves consciously and preparing for a new opportunity, a new period, of earthly existence and effort. Such a knowledge of the true laws enables us to be prepared for the future regardless of transition, and it makes us realize that there is nothing in transition to be feared and nothing to be regretted if we live in accordance with the highest ideals of the Cosmic.

The doctrines of reincarnation assure us that if we follow the Great Master, living the true Christian spirit, or follow the highest teachings of our religion whatever it may be, we will earn certain rewards that will strengthen us and prepare us for another life in which we can earn additional rewards and reach a higher state of development. Through these continued existences on earth we can gradually attain that perfection and that degree of Christian spirit in our consciousness that will make us ready to stand before the Great Judge and receive the Highest Benediction.

The person who has accepted the doctrines of reincarnation knows truly that there is no death. He is not one who sings the songs and proclaims "there is no death" and yet fears it in his heart, fighting against the decrees of nature when the time comes for the casting off of the old and worn-out body and the taking on of a new life. He is cheerful and happy in the knowledge that as he sows today, so shall he reap; that he will suffer for the evil he has done, but is given every opportunity to compensate and to redeem himself and live again in accordance with the highest ideals. Wherever we find one who understands these doctrines, there we will find one who is cheerful, happy, successful, godlike, kind, tolerant, and considerate. But more than anything else you will find that such a person has no fear of the future, nor fear of transition, and no dread of so-called death.

CHAPTER 19

QUESTIONS AND ANSWERS

It may be more interesting to cover the usual objections and questions relating to the doctrines of reincarnation by selecting the principal ones from a mass of correspondence and putting the answers with them.

*   *   *

Question: Why is it that we do not hear more about reincarnation from eminent or well-known scientists and clergymen? Does this not indicate that such persons do not approve of the doctrines?

Answer: Clergymen or others who are the accepted representatives of religious creeds or movements which do not include the doctrines of reincarnation can hardly be expected to promote such doctrines or endorse them, regardless of what their personal opinions may be. On the other hand, many eminent clergymen and scientists have endorsed the principles of the doctrines of reincarnation. Scientists, especially, have often made public statements in this regard, and so have many prominent and successful businessmen. Typical of both of these classes are Arthur Conan Doyle and Henry Ford. We must remember, however, that few people wear their religions on their sleeves and very few, indeed, desire to proclaim their personal religious or philosophical beliefs; the mere silence on the part of any person in regard to such beliefs in nowise indicates the true thoughts that may be in his mind. If you can succeed in having prominent persons tell you in confidence their personal opinions and beliefs you may be surprised at their comments.

Question: Why do you not publish a list of all of the prominent people or well-known thinkers who have endorsed the doctrines of reincarnation?

Answer: Simply because such a list would be unfair unless it were nearly complete, and a complete list would make an entire volume of a large size, which few would care to read. Secondly, the doctrines of reincarnation are not offered or presented to anyone as something which should be accepted because of eminent endorsement. Many of the most notable fallacies and unsound theories which have had popular acceptance were at one time offered to the public solely through eminent scientific or ecclesiastical endorsement. Thousands have been burned at the stake or slaughtered in their homes because they refused to accept doctrines or dogmas which were eminently endorsed and promoted by the representatives of those who endorsed them. Yet, these very principles and dogmas were later found to be untrue.

Millions of persons in the past have accepted on faith the ideas and beliefs of others only to find that they were just as truly misled by such eminent endorsement as by their own judgment. The doctrines of reincarnation have not spread throughout the world to become important guides in the lives of millions through endorsement, but through the common-sense, logical reasoning on the part of the men and women who have given their own thoughts to the mysteries of life and to the analyzing of the doctrines. If your own good judgment cannot convince you of the soundness of the doctrines of reincarnation, you should not accept them on the strength of someone else's faith in them or someone else's endorsement of them.

Question: What becomes of the idea, or belief, in the resurrection of the body, if the doctrines of reincarnation are true?

Answer: If it is true that there will come a day when all of the physical bodies in dissolution in all parts of the world will have their elements drawn together and the dust of their bones restored and the cells of the flesh reestablished into physical forms again and arise from the graves to ascend into the heavens, there is nothing in the doctrines of reincarnation to refute it. The personality or soul of a person may reincarnate a thousand times and still dwell eventually in heaven and await the resurrection of the last physical body possessed by it. Whatever is true will be made manifest, and if the doctrines of reincarnation are true they cannot be contrary to any other doctrines that are true.

Question: What about twins? If two bodies are born at practically the same minute, are there two segments of the soul or two personalities in the bodies, or just one?

Answer: Physiologically and biologically the bodies of some twins are "identical" and had their origin in one conception. The same soul personality that was intended for one body would then be divided between the two, and would reside in the two bodies, and manifest through them throughout life. This is why some twins have the same inner natures, the same tendencies, talents, and emotional characteristics even when the outer, physical countenance is slightly different. When transition comes, the soul in the bodies of such twins returns to the Cosmic as one soul personality and may or may not enter the bodies of twins again. There are records of many a person who had found in the peculiar complex nature of his personality, and in the psychic functioning of his soul, that in a previous incarnation his soul personality had been divided between two bodies of twins and had accumulated many strange experiences in life.

When one of the twins passes through transition ahead of the other, the soul with its personality of the one that has passed on unites with the one still living. The continued contact between the two inner selves of the twins, whereby each is constantly conscious of the thoughts and emotions of the other, and often senses even injuries to the physical body of the other, or suffers similar disorders and annoyances, proves how closely related the soul personality in each of them actually is.

Question: What effect has suicide on the evolution of the soul?

Answer: The wilful interference with any of nature's laws creates a karmic condition which the personality of the individual must adjust through compensation. The wilful and sudden ending of human life with the arbitrary separation of the soul from the body plunges the soul personality into an abyss of darkness for many days and weeks, in which condition the personality suffers intensely and is "earthbound" for a long period. The regret for the act is keenly realized and felt by the personality throughout its entire cosmic existence, and its reincarnation is always in a body which will have to suffer certain trials and tribulations of life until it learns the error of what it has done and makes proper compensation. The idea that suicide will bring an end to any of our earthly sufferings, trials, and tribulations is the most absurd idea that man has ever held. No matter how intense may be our earthly sufferings, or how despondent we may be, all of this is nothing as compared with the suffering that is immediately realized after transition through suicide.

Question: Since Jesus did not definitely proclaim his belief in reincarnation, and my church does not preach it, I cannot believe that the doctrines are true. Is not the old religion of the Christian church good enough for me?

Answer: What do you mean by *the old religion?* The Christian religion has been evolving and passing through stages of modification ever since Jesus first proclaimed it to his disciples. Many of the things which you hear preached in your church today, and which you have accepted during your lifetime, were unheard of and unknown in the Christian religion some centuries ago. The Christian religion is a living, evolving guide in men's lives, and it evolves and keeps alive through man's continued elaboration of his interpretation and understanding of that which Jesus taught. There are many things which Jesus taught his disciples which are not preached in the Christian religion because they would not apply and could not apply to our modern ways of living, and there are many things in the Christian doctrines of today which were not expounded by Jesus, nor contained in the Christian teachings, until many centuries after the ascension of Jesus. There are, undoubtedly, many principles and doctrines of your religion acceptable to you today which your great grandparents would have criticized and would have said were modernistic, man-made, and unwarranted.

You are mistaken when you think that Jesus did not show any belief in or acceptance of the doctrines of reincarnation. Your minister, or someone else, may tell you that he did not, but if you will read certain chapters of this book again and read your Bible carefully, you will find that Jesus did admit the soundness of the doctrines of reincarnation. However, if your present religion is perfectly satisfactory to you, and you can find joy and peace in knowing and accepting only some of the laws of life while you ignore and turn your back upon others which are equally important, then this is your privilege and you should not attempt to force yourself to change your attitude.

Question: I think it is horrifying to believe that the soul must go through all of these periods of earthly experiences, suffering, and trials. Since the soul is divine and a part of the God essence, why should it require earthly experiences to help it reach perfection?

Answer: The fact of the matter is that the soul *is here* in the physical body in contact with earthly trials and tribulations, suffering an earthly existence, through the decree of God. We cannot get around the fact that God has ordained this. It may be horrifying for you to think that a part of God's consciousness is here on the earth, associated with sordid things, but as a matter of course this fact is true, and God alone is responsible for it. That being so, why should it appear horrifying that the soul and personality should have more than one opportunity to exist on earth, and perhaps have several opportunities to exist here in better circumstances and under better conditions, with more happiness and joy than maybe found in just one lifetime?

You seem to assume that the doctrines of reincarnation are responsible for the soul of man being imprisoned in a physical body here on earth. This is not true. The doctrines of reincarnation simply attempt to explain *why* this divine fact was decreed by God. If you take the doctrines of reincarnation and destroy them and wipe them out of existence, you still have to explain why the consciousness or soul of God was extended into a physical body to reside here on earth and go through trials and tribulations which the soul of God would not require. If you can answer that question with a more logical doctrine than that of reincarnation, you will solve the greatest problem that has confronted thinking men and women since the dawn of civilization.

But remember the answer given by the average clergyman that "it is the will of God and not for us to understand," is not an answer but an evasion. We may not be able to understand all about it but we certainly understand enough to know that the divine consciousness of God was purposely projected into the physical body here on earth, and while here this divine soul of God is in contact with sorrowful and perplexing conditions. To say that we cannot understand does not wipe out of our minds the question, and does not answer your own question. A better answer must be found, and the only better one that has ever been found is in the doctrines presented in this book.

Question: Do you not realize that your doctrines of reincarnation do away with hell and purgatory as established in the Christian religion?

Answer: I know this one fact, that the Christian religion did not originally contain any dogmas about hell and purgatory.

I challenge you to find any place in the New Testament where Jesus has spoken about purgatory or described hell in the manner in which it is presented today in the Christian religion. Therefore, please do not try to attribute hell and purgatory to Jesus, regardless of what your clergyman may say. Both of these conditions or places are additions to the Christian doctrines made long after the life of Jesus. But, again, I say if they are true, then no other truth can destroy them. If there is a hell or purgatory into which the soul and personalities of man must pass or dwell after transition, it would not in any way interfere with the rebirth of the soul and personality after these had been purged or cleansed in hell or purgatory.

Question: Why should we bother about the subject of reincarnation at all? Is not life just as happy without knowing about all this?

Answer: Very likely life is just as happy for some without any knowledge as it is for those who have a great amount of knowledge. Why do you read the Bible, or go to church, or study anything about God's laws? You will probably live just as long without such knowledge but you certainly will not be as happy. While you are in perfect health and seemingly far from the day of transition you may safely say that you have no interest in what happens after your transition, but there may come a day when you will become profoundly interested in knowing something about the future and when you will find great consolation and peace in any knowledge regarding the hereafter. Fortunately, the larger part of the world finds its joy and happiness in knowledge, and the more knowledge and the greater understanding of life and its principles, the more happiness and contentment. The more that anyone knows about the real principles of his existence here and hereafter, the more happy and successful and perfect the life of that person will be.

Question: I do not like the thought of coming back again in some unknown body and having to live again through all the suffering of this life. I would rather dwell in eternal peace when this life is over.

Answer: It is not a matter of what we would like, but of what is the law. When you are born again you will come into this earthly life just as you did in your present incarnation, knowing nothing about your past existence and filled with the joy and happiness of being alive and among the living. If you are one of the unusual persons who find no joy at all in life, and find nothing in life to make it worth while, you are of the type that has failed to bring joy and happiness into the lives of others and you are reaping only what you have sown. You will live again whether you want to or not, and you will continue to be reborn on this earth until you make the utmost of your life and find real joy and happiness in being among the living and in accomplishing much for others. Do not think that by ignoring the laws of reincarnation and claiming that you do not believe in them that you will prevent their operation or manifestation in your life. Therefore, so long as you will be born again and will live again, is it not better that you should know something about it and prepare yourself for it?

Question: What determines the nature of the soul for any specific body that is to be born?

Answer: The determining factor is Karma. A personality awaiting rebirth which has certain karmic compensations to make or certain karmic adjustments to make will be cosmically directed toward an unborn body, which, by the nature of its environment, family associations, locality, nationality, etc., will provide the opportunities for the soul personality to carry on with its Karma. A soul personality that is awaiting rebirth and which has in its make-up the talents and abilities for music or art because of previous experience in these lines, will be directed toward an unborn body that will provide the opportunities for the expression of these talents and abilities.

Let us say, for instance, that there is a soul personality in the Cosmic awaiting rebirth which should continue its musical career and become more famous or more perfect in music. It will be directed toward an unborn body, the parents of which will be inclined by their own desires and tastes to give the child further musical education and provide the opportunities for its development along this line. If, for instance, an expectant mother desires to have a child who will be famous as a musician, and throughout the prenatal period concentrates her mind upon attracting to her unborn child the soul of a musician, and the father likewise agrees with the wife that the child that comes to them will be given every opportunity to have a musical career, the Cosmic will direct toward the unborn body the soul personality of one inclined toward or partially perfected in music.

The same would be true of any other special talent or abilities. In determining into which body a soul should enter, the Cosmic takes into consideration what the soul personality will accomplish in its next incarnation and also what certain unborn bodies may provide in the way of opportunities for these karmic conditions to manifest. An unborn body about to be born in an environment of poverty, ignorance, and physical as well as material handicaps, will have directed toward it the soul personality that requires these earthly conditions, in order to learn certain lessons and to overcome and master certain conditions. The prenatal influences of the parents, and especially of the mother, have a very definite effect with the Cosmic in determining which personality or soul essence shall enter the body of the unborn.

Question: Has the soul any free choice in the selection of the physical vehicle for its next earthly expression?

Answer: The soul personality dwelling in the Cosmic awaiting rebirth does not have any free choice in the selection of the body into which it is to be incarnated. It may be attracted toward certain unborn bodies by a previous relationship, a sympathetic understanding, or some other sentimental or psychic condition, but unless this attraction fits in with the cosmic scheme, such an attraction will not decide the matter at all. The greatest influence outside of the Cosmic Mind is in the influence of parents and especially that of the mother. Parents who purposely conceive of a child with the intention of providing a vehicle for a beautiful, spiritual soul, in order that a great character and personality may be incarnated on earth and accomplish great things, will undoubtedly attract to the unborn body the very kind of soul personality they have in mind.

The more holy and sacred is the relationship of human conception and the higher the ideals held by the parents for the future of the unborn body, and the more definite their visualization of the type of character they desire in the child, the more surely will the Cosmic attend to the fulfillment of their wishes. Considering that the Cosmic at all times possesses in its Oversoul thousands upon thousands of personalities awaiting rebirth, each of a distinctly different type with a distinctly different karmic future and distinctly different tendencies and abilities, it is easy to understand how the Cosmic can direct toward any unborn body the type and character of personality that the parents may desire.

Question: What effect upon the future child have the destructive thoughts of a mother or father who does not want a child and tries to prevent its birth?

Answer: In such a case we would have a situation the very reverse of that stated above. When a mother is determined not to have a child, and from the moment of conception attempts to destroy the embryo or prevent the development and birth of the body, her mind is filled with two strong emotions. First, that of hatred and enmity toward the body that is being created and the body that is coming, and, secondly, the thought of murder and destruction. She will attract to the unborn body the soul personality that must fulfill certain karmic conditions of its own and at the same time assist in teaching the parents the error of their thoughts. Therefore, a personality that is of an unsympathetic and unkindly type, given to destructive acts, may be directed toward this unborn body, and during this child's adolescence the parents will realize the error of their thinking and will appreciate the fact that they have reaped as they have sown, while the child itself will grow into manhood and have an opportunity of purging itself of the evil tendencies it has and be prepared for a better and more noble birth in the next incarnation.

Question: What effect does the education and social position of parents have upon the selection of a soul personality for their unborn child?

Answer: Parents who are in good social position and well educated will have directed toward them, or may attract to them, the personality of a soul that requires the opportunities for karmic adjustment which social position and education will provide; or such a soul personality as must learn the lessons of life through being born into a family of affluence and suddenly find these things taken away and a life of poverty remaining. A soul personality that in a previous incarnation had bitterly hated all persons of wealth and social position would be cosmically directed to be born in a family of wealth and influence in order that it might learn that all such persons are not evil minded and unworthy of esteem.

A soul personality that in a previous incarnation had freely and happily given away everything of its small earthly wealth to help in every possible humanitarian activity, and gladly suffered in want in order to help others, might be cosmically directed in the next incarnation to a body born in an environment of wealth so that it could continue to do its humanitarian work without limitation. If, in this new incarnation, it failed to continue to do the good it had done when living in want, it would not be born again in wealth, but after having had an opportunity to distribute wealth to the needy and having applied it selfishly, it would be born in its next incarnation in an environment of poverty or want in order to be impressed once again with certain values and conditions of life.

Question: Is it possible for an expectant mother to attract to her unborn child the soul personality of a child she had earlier in her life and which was taken away through transition?

Answer: This is possible, although the mother might not know for many years that she had succeeded in attracting the same soul personality for a second time. There are instances on record where a mother has finally recognized in her second child the character and personality of a child that she had many years before and which passed through transition at the age of twelve or fifteen. Such instances, of course, require a short period on the cosmic plane between births and are an exception to the general cycle of rebirth, but for some cosmic reason the exception is made.

Question: Do the thoughts of the mother during the prenatal period have any effect upon not only the personality of the soul that is to come to the child, but upon the child's physical body and sex?

Answer: If the prenatal influences of the mother begin soon enough after conception, or really start at the time of conception, it is possible for these thoughts of the mother and father to determine the sex and the general physiological characteristics of the future child as well as the spiritual characteristics. The Greeks were famous for their knowledge and efficiency in the application of such knowledge along this line, but the art of prenatalism has almost become lost. There are some organizations in the world, including the Rosicrucians, who retain and promulgate private instructions and knowledge regarding this subject. The degree of success attained through prenatal wishes depends upon the efficiency of the methods used by the parents and the use of the proper degree of concentration.

Question: Is there any tendency upon the part of the Cosmic to continue the incarnation of certain soul personalities in the same family lines of generation?

Answer: Nothing has been found in any of the tests and revelations connected with research on this subject indicating that this is so. After a soul personality enters the Cosmic through transition it loses all of its association and connection with its physiological or material, earthly relations. Family blood and family trees are matters of the physical body and not of the soul personality, and in the Cosmic there are no such things as physical, earthly relationships.

Question: What is meant by "carrying over" something from a previous incarnation?

Answer: Usually it is said that when a person manifests early in this life some very distinct tastes or tendencies or dislikes and repulsions, he has carried these things over from a previous existence. It is also said that persons who have a fear of the water, or of fire, or sharp instruments, or of certain locations or positions, have also carried these things over from the past. It has been found that many of the strongest likes and dislikes in our present personality, and especially those which manifest themselves in our childhood or youth, are the outstanding points of our personality in its last incarnation, and that these things had such a dominant place in our life that they easily rise now from the memory of the secondary personality and have become parts of our present character.

Question: Is it true that the things which we were most concerned about during the last hours of our life in a previous existence become dominating factors in our thinking and acting in the present existence?

Answer: From very careful investigations which have been made it has been quite conclusively proved that those thoughts which occupied our minds most strongly, and with profound concern, during the last conscious moments before transition in a previous existence will become guide-posts to our thinking in the present incarnation. A man or woman whose last conscious thoughts were centered around regrets for having performed or committed some sin or act of injury to another, and whose last conscious thinking was concerned with a desire to be able to undo or make recompense and compensation for these acts, will undoubtedly carry into the next incarnation the unquenchable desire to do something for those who are found in similar predicaments.

As a hypothetical example let us say that a person in his last hours regretted the fact that he had at some time in his life performed an injustice against a widow with two children by robbing them of their rightful inheritance, and he desired above all things that he might live a few hours longer and make recompense and undo the wrong he did. If this all-absorbing desire was still in his mind when transition came, it would be so registered in the consciousness of his personality that in the next incarnation it would be uppermost in all of his inward reflections or passive meditations. It would seem then as a strange and unquenchable desire to locate widows with children or persons in similar conditions who were in great want, or who were in serious predicaments through the wrongs of another, and try to alleviate their suffering or do something to help them in adjusting their affairs.

This desire might manifest early in childhood or youth in the form of a sympathetic emotion which would rise uncontrollably whenever the story or facts of such a situation were brought before him, and even though this person later on attained only moderate circumstances in life he would be found at various times attempting in some way to help those of this class who were in such situations. This explains why many persons, even those who are living a life or evil or crime, often have deep-seated emotional tendencies of a charitable or humanitarian nature. Very often these persons look upon such tendencies in their nature as weaknesses, and they frankly admit that there is a "baby" nature within them which they cannot restrict and correct, and which cries and is moved by certain forms of sorrows or wrongs in life. Many of our strongest emotions or impulses toward human conditions and relationships, which were discovered in our nature early in life, are unquestionably carried over from the past.

Question: Is it possible that a person who lived a life of crime and who always sought an opportunity to injure others, and who passed through transition suddenly in the height of his ambitions for crime, would "carry over" into the next incarnation these tendencies and desires to do wrong and injury?

Answer: The purpose of the soul's temporary residence in the cosmic realm between incarnations is for the cleansing and purification of the evil tendencies in the personality. A person whose transition occurred in the very height of crime activity, with the personality held in the ambition of crime, would not come into life again with these same tendencies. Before his rebirth his personality would not only have been purged of these evil desires and tendencies, but the suffering through regret, and the lessons learned while in the cosmic realm, would have taught the personality the error of such thinking and would have substituted the desire to live properly. There would still remain, however, the karmic debt to make compensation for the crimes previously committed. Therefore, such a person would be born again with no desires to do evil, but rather with strong desires to live properly. Nevertheless, the need to pay the karmic debt would force this person to pass through many forms of suffering, injury, and sorrow at the hands of others similar to that caused in the lives of other persons in his previous existence.

This person now attempting to live correctly and being free entirely from any evil thoughts or evil desires and ambitions, always doing what was right, would nevertheless find himself suffering and in sorrow as though he had actually committed many crimes and many evil acts in his present life. This is why so many persons who are truly trying to live a good life, and who are really idealistic in their desires and plans for living, wonder why they are often plunged into sorrow, want, and misery like unto those who are now living lives of evil and crime. They say, "I am trying to do my best, living the best I know how, doing no injury to anyone, and yet every now and then I am reduced to want, denied those things I desire the most, and made to suffer like those who do evil. Does it pay, therefore, to live rightly and think rightly when one has to suffer like those who live wrongly?"

If these persons understood that the sorrow and misery in their lives is the adjustment that they are making for the past, and thereby cleansing the spirit and making it wholesome for a future life of happiness, and by their present attempts to live correctly they are guaranteeing a life of joy and abundance in the future, they would not become so discouraged and would not be puzzled by the seeming paradoxes of life.

Question: Why is it that so many persons who are living in evil ways and actually doing wrong unto others seem to be so happy and enjoy not only all the necessities and many of the luxuries of life, but apparently escape all punishment here and all detection in their evil ways?

Answer: First, let me say that in most cases we make serious errors in our judgment of the success, happiness, and prosperity of persons who are engaged in crime or evil living. From our distant or external point of view it may seem that these persons are happy, or prospering in their crimes and avoiding dedication and punishment. The fact that the Cosmic is conscious of our wrongs, however, and that they are not escaping cosmic detection and inevitable punishment, shows how we may be mistaken in thinking that human detection has been evaded. Most certainly we may be greatly mistaken in believing that these persons are prospering in financial, social, or other ways through their crimes, for it is a fact that very few criminals, even those who have in the height of their careers obtained enormous fortunes of worldly possessions, have ever passed away in even moderate worldly circumstances; and usually the close of their lives finds them in abject poverty and want, along with social rejection and the scorn of their companions.

The average criminal who has eventually found redemption through his own thinking, or through religion or personal help and guidance, has admitted that in dollars and cents paid to avoid detection and cover the crimes or secure legal advice, and to escape the revenge of his blackmailing associates, and in hours of worry, hiding, mental torment, and inner condemnation, it had cost him more than he ever secured through his crime. The criminal's prosperity of today, or of this month or year, may be his karmic load of tomorrow or the following year. His outward appearance of enjoying the things of life may be the coating of veneer which he must assume in order to escape public detection. Neither you nor I can ever tell what such a person suffers in the privacy of his own life. But, even though the person who lives in evil should prosper in the material things of life, there is no question about the *inevitable price* that he must pay and suffer in the purging process during the cosmic period and in the karmic compensation process in his next life among other mortals.

It is only our man-made process of punishing a criminal or evildoer here and now, and in like manner unto his crime, that makes us think that those who are continuing in evil without *immediate* punishment are escaping punishment altogether. As stated elsewhere in this book, the cosmic laws of compensation do not seek to punish a man on a basis of "an eye for an eye and a tooth for a tooth," nor to revengefully make man suffer for his evildoing, but seek to bring about such reactions for his crime as will sometime, in some manner, most propitiously and efficiently cause him to realize the error of his ways and aid him to correct them, and give him an opportunity to compensate for them and otherwise find redemption and salvation. The keynote to the cosmic law of Karma is *regeneration* rather than *punishment.*

Question: Is it true that when a person is under the influence of a powerful drug and is in a deep unconscious state, the soul leaves the body and wanders about in space and may not return? Is it also true that in such circumstances the soul of some person also wandering in space may come back into the wrong body?

Answer: Both of these questions can be easily and quickly cast aside with the explanation that the soul never leaves the physical body and breaks its contact with the body except at "death" or transition. That being true, the other fanciful beliefs regarding the soul wandering in space and getting lost are seen to be absurdities. The only difference between the state called *death* and the deep sleep or a trance condition is the separation of soul and body. When this separation takes place and the soul is no longer in contact with its body, we have the unique condition called *transition* or *death.* There is no other condition precisely like it. A person, therefore, must be either living or non-living so far as the soul in the body is concerned.

What occurs during the period of sleep or unconsciousness through drugs of any kind is of a purely psychological nature and has very little to do with the soul. The state is primarily physiological with its related effect upon the psychic conditions. The soul does not wander in space at such times but remains in the body. The ego may extend itself and its consciousness may appear to wander in space by making wide and various contacts through its extension, but it never becomes separated from the body. Furthermore, there are no souls wandering in space to become lost, and there is no such thing as a lost soul slipping back into a body to which it has not been cosmically assigned. These sorts of ideas are examples of the strange teachings issued by some mystical schools and are limited only by the daydreams and imagination of the authors of such teachings.

Question: Are there any reports on record of persons who have been on the borderline of transition and returned to life to explain any strange experiences?

Answer: Yes, there are many such reports and the only evidential value that lies in these reports is the similarity of statements made by persons in various parts of the world who had no way of knowing what others had reported in similar circumstances.

A typical case of this kind is that of a young man of twenty-four who suffered a relapse after an operation in a hospital, and for several days continued to sink in vitality and consciousness until the doctor and nurses were waiting the ultimate transition. One afternoon, at a little after two o'clock, when two nurses, a physician, and four friends were seated around the bedside of the semiconscious patient, he suddenly relaxed and gave every indication of having passed into the so-called death state. As the nurses proceeded to cover the body and arrange the hands and arms in a proper position, all in the semilighted room were surprised to see a white haze float upward from the body for a few feet, and then assume a vertical position and descend, to remain over in one of the corners of the bedroom. Everyone rose to his feet and stood spellbound, silent, and reverential. Not a word was spoken for a full long minute. Then the physician recommended that the body be removed from the room for the usual care given to the dead.

As the nurses again attempted to touch the physical body, the misty haze in the corner of the room trembled or shook violently so that its light waves seemed to undulate in a peculiar manner. This action was so definite that everyone in the room except the physician suggested that the body be left on the bed for a while and that tests be made to see whether "death" had actually occurred. Every scientific test was made during the next fifteen minutes and the nurses agreed with the physician that there was no possibility of life in the body. Again, however, the strange misty haze in the corner of the room, which was almost six feet in height and about the width of a human body, trembled and seemed agitated by the attempt to remove the body from the bed.

One of the friends present—who was a student of the Rosicrucian teachings and well versed in these matters—suggested that the room be darkened by drawing down the shades at the windows and closing the door for a few minutes in order to see if the misty light or haze in the corner of the room had any real significance. The physician agreed with some reluctance and all the persons in the room stood in a corner opposite to the misty haze, so as to have a better view of it. As the eyes become accustomed to the darkness of the room it was noticed that a very thin and hovering cord or beam of hazy light seemed to stretch across the bed and unite the misty haze in the corner with the physical body on the bed. This was definitely seen even by the physician and the nurses, who agreed that it was an unusual sight. It was suggested then that this might indicate that consciousness had not entirely left the body and that there was still some life in it.

The idea was proposed then that all remain seated for a while and see if there was any development of a significant nature. The physician explained that if the body was lifeless, minutes should not be lost in performing the usual preparations upon the body in making it ready for burial. Of course, this meant the draining of the fluids from the body and the injection of the embalming fluids. At each suggestion that this be done, the misty haze in the corner became agitated as though protesting against the suggestion. It was this possibility that gradually dawned upon the consciousness of those assembled, for it did appear that each time the approach was made to the body to remove it, there was a reaction as of protest on the part of the misty haze.

After about twenty more minutes had passed, those assembled in the room became conscious of the fact that the thin beam of light that united the body with the haze in the corner was widening or becoming thicker or more brilliant. At first, this was attributed to the adjustment of the eyes to the darkness of the room, but soon it was noticed that the misty haze in the corner was being absorbed into the beam and that in this manner the whole hazy figure in the corner of the room was being drawn toward the physical body on the bed. In what was considered to be about four minutes, the entire misty haze in the corner had disappeared and was hovering over the physical body and was gradually beginning to lower itself into the physical form. In another two or three minutes, there was no indication of the misty haze in any part of the room. The shades at the windows were lifted and in the soft light of the room further tests were made of the physical body. Indications of life or vitality were then discovered, and immediately methods were used to restore or strengthen the vitality to its greatest degree. In a little less than an hour breathing started, and there was a return of temperature to parts of the body.

By seven o'clock that evening, with the same nurses and visiting friends still in attendance and with only an absence of one hour on the part of the physician, the young man regained consciousness sufficiently to open his eyes and to announce that he was "all right." Three other physicians and several nurses of the staff were invited to the room to watch the procedure. The young man regained consciousness sufficiently to sit up in bed before ten o'clock in the evening, and to make a few comments. His only statement at that time was that he had been outside of his body and had watched the whole procedure in the room, but knew that he was still connected in a strange way with the physical body on the bed and that he had done his outmost to prevent them from doing anything that would have severed that connection.

The next day, he told his story of how he had passed through a strange change whereby his consciousness or his real self with which he did his thinking and realizing had floated out of his body and remained in the corner of the room, being pushed to that corner by some peculiar emanations of the physical bodies of those present and yet held fast to his own physical body by an extension of consciousness, or something that enabled him to feel every touch made on the physical body that was lying on the bed. He said that his first desire was to keep on going off into space, for he heard beautiful music, saw endless spaces of clouds with brilliant lights, and saw many forms like his own with emanations of peace and happiness. He said that this temptation to go off into space and not return to the physical body was checked only by the strange pull toward the physical form and that every time the nurses laid their hands on his physical body or attempted to move it in its position, it gave him a shock like an electric shock.

The hundreds of other things that he described later on coincided with similar statements made by others who had passed through the same experience in various parts of the world. These experiences have no place in this book, since they deal with purely personal impressions and cannot be verified except by those who have passed through similar experiences. The only positive evidence that can be extracted from such experiences is that which the nurses, physician, and friends saw with their own eyes, and from the fact that the body had been found to be so lifeless that no life would register on the most delicate instruments, and yet in less than eight hours afterwards, the man was alive again and able to sit up and talk.

Question: Is it true that in the so-called spiritualistic seances held in darkened rooms the souls of departed persons return to earth and clothe themselves with a material form of such a nature that no physiological difference can be found between these materialized souls and an actual, earthly, physical body?

Answer: It is an absolute fact that the soul of an individual does not return to earth except to reincarnate again, and therefore does not float around in space and visit seance rooms, or psychic laboratories or research circles at any time. It is also an absolute fact that the soul cannot take on mortality, or physical form, except through incarnation in a physical body in the form of an infant. To explain what *apparently* takes place in a seance room and what *actually* takes place would require a large volume.

It is possible for the consciousness of a departed soul to project its mentality to a distant place on earth, just as the consciousness or mentality of a person living on earth can project itself to a distant point and make itself sensed by those who may be properly attuned to receive such impressions. But this is not a projection of the soul, nor is it a materialization of the soul, as the students of spiritualistic phenomena claim through their misunderstanding of the real principles involved. I do not mean to say that certain things do not occur in a seance room, which will give the impression of a materialized soul, but I do mean to say that it is not what they believe it to be and, therefore, not what they claim it to be. The soul does not materialize itself, and it does not become clothed with a physical form except through incarnation.

Question: Is it true that the most intimate contacts made with departed souls are those which are made in the privacy of one's own home or in private circumstances, rather than in general seances or research assemblies?

Answer: This is absolutely true and it explains why groups of scientists, proceeding to investigate psychic phenomena in a materialistic, cold scientific manner, do not have the experiences and the convincing results that have been experienced by millions of persons in the privacy of their own home, or when alone, and in proper mental, spiritual, and psychic circumstances.

We may well understand that if it is possible for a loved one, who has departed, to project his or her mental consciousness to the earth plane in order to communicate some consoling thoughts or spiritual knowledge of a personal nature, it would be done preferably in circumstances that are reverential and personal rather than in circumstances of a public or scientific nature. It is also true that the one most concerned here on earth in such an experience and who desires such a spiritual contact must, through reverential sacredness and spiritual attunement, lift up the consciousness part way to meet the consciousness that is being projected toward the earth. It is this mutual attunement of a truly sacred nature that makes possible the many thousands of personal, private, intimate contacts never duplicated in public, or scientific laboratories, or seances. Rosicrucians and others well versed in the true spiritual and cosmic laws of the universe, and knowing man's spiritual and cosmic qualifications, attune themselves through study and experiment to make such contacts easily and efficiently.

INDEX

Purgatory, 107, 119, 153,
201-202
Purification, 106, 116, 211

R

Radiations,
Vibratory, 145
Realm,
Cosmic, 143, 147, 149, 152,
211
Heavenly, 152
Spiritual, 141, 144, 147, 150,
151, 153
Rebirth (See also Reincarnation)
Rebirths, 112-119, 135-137,
141-142, 207-208, 212
Period, 135-139
Redemption, 214
Regeneration, 215
Regret, 198, 210-211
Reincarnation, 9-10, 17-24, 27,
34-35, 67-69, 72, 74, 84-98,
101, 103-113, 115-121, 134,
138, 141, 151-153, 164-165,
175, 177-178, 189, 191-193,
195-198, 201-203
Church, 199-200
Cycles, 152, 184
Religions
Christian, 37, 39, 98, 109,
120, 193, 199, 201
Jewish, 37, 39, 98-99, 103
Occidental, 98
Oriental, 41
Western, 35, 97-98
Revenge, 62
Rhinoceros, 166

Rosicrucians, 147, 149, 208,
222
Teachings, 217
Royal Asiatic Society, 102

S

Salvation, 65, 71, 81
Savior, 112
Science, Materialistic, 57-59
Scriptures, 14
(See Writings)
Seances, 156, 220-221
Segments, Unseparated, 123
Self, 55
Inner, 26, 28, 51-55, 148-
150, 155, 160, 198
Self-conscious Self
(see Subliminal Self)
Seth, 107
Simon Magus, 106
Simon Peter, 118
Sin, 64, 105-107, 111, 119, 153,
173, 191
Original, 63
Snakes, 166
Soul, 16, 20-23, 26, 28-48,
57-61, 69, 83, 85, 103-107,
110, 112-113, 115, 123-124,
127-136, 141-145, 147-152,
173, 197-198, 200-201, 204-
207, 215-216, 220-221
Animal, 165-168, 170
Consciousness, 48, 124
Cycles, 136
Evolution, 85, 87, 95-96
Immortality, 30-31, 84-85
Incarnation, 34-35, 43, 49,
142

THE ROSICRUCIAN ORDER
Purpose and Work of the Order

The Rosicrucian Order, AMORC, is a philosophical and initiatic tradition. As students progress in their studies, they are initiated into the next level or degree.

Rosicrucians are men and women around the world who study the laws of nature in order to live in harmony with them. Individuals study the Rosicrucian lessons in the privacy of their own homes on subjects such as the nature of the soul, developing intuition, classical Greek philosophy, energy centers in the body, and self-healing techniques.

The Rosicrucian tradition encourages each student to discover the wisdom, compassion, strength, and peace that already reside within each of us.

www.rosicrucian.org